THE
HERSCHEL
HOBBS
COMMENTARY

STUDYING
ADULT
LIFE AND WORK
LESSONS

by

HERSCHEL H. HOBBS
&
ROSS H. McLAREN

SUMMER
June–August 1997
Volume 29, Number 4

ROSS H. McLAREN
Biblical Studies Specialist

Carolyn Gregory
Production Specialist

Stephen Smith
Graphic Designer

Carla Dickerson
Technical Specialist

Send questions/comments to
Ross H. McLaren, editor
127 9th Ave., North
Nashville, TN 37234-0175

Management Personnel

Rick Edwards, *Manager*
Adult Biblical Studies Section
Louis B. Hanks, *Director,*
Biblical Studies Department
Ken Marler, *Team Leader*
Age Group Field Services Team
_____ , *Team Leader*
Age Group Ministry Design and
Resources Team

BILL L. TAYLOR, *Director*
Bible Teaching-Reaching Division

ACKNOWLEDGMENTS.–We believe
the Bible has God for its author, salvation for its end, and truth, without
any mixture of error, for its matter.
The 1963 statement of *The Baptist
Faith and Message* is our doctrinal
guideline.

Unless otherwise indicated, all
Scripture quotations are from the
King James Version. This translation
is available in a Holman Bible and can
be ordered through Baptist Book
Stores or Lifeway Christian Stores.
Quotations marked ASV are from the
American Standard Version. Copyright ©
1901 by Thomas Nelson & Sons. Quotations
marked Beck are from *The Holy Bible in the
Language of Today* by William F. Beck. Copyright © Mrs. William F. Beck, 1976. Published
by Holman Bible Publishers. Used by permission. Scripture quotations identified as CEV
are from the *Contemporary English Version.*
Copyright © American Bible Society 1991,
1992. Used by permission. Verses marked
TLB are taken from *The Living Bible.* Copyright © Tyndale House Publishers, Wheaton,
Illinois, 1971. Used by permission. Quotations
marked MLB or Berkeley Version are from
*The Modern Language Bible, The New Berke-
ley Version.* Copyright 1945, 1959 © by Zondervan Publishing House. Used by permission. Quotations marked Moffatt are from *The
Bible: A New Translation* by James Moffatt.
Copyright © 1935 by Harper-Collins Publishers. Quotations marked NAB are from the
New American Bible. Copyright © P. J.
Kenedy & Sons, New York, 1970. Passages
marked NASB are from the *New American
Standard Bible: 1995 Update.* © The Lock-
man Foundation, 1960, 1962, 1963, 1968,
1971, 1972, 1973, 1975, 1977, 1995. Used by
permission. Quotations marked NCV are from
The Holy Bible, *New Century Version.* Copyright © 1987, 1988, 1991 by Word Publishing,
Dallas, Texas 75039. Used by permission.
Quotations marked NEB are from *The New
English Bible.* Copyright © The Delegates of
the Oxford University Press and the Syndics
of the Cambridge University Press, 1961,
1970. Reprinted by permission. Quotations
marked NIV are from the Holy Bible, *New
International Version,* copyright © 1973, 1978,
1984 by International Bible Society. This
translation is available in a Holman Bible
and can be ordered through Baptist Book
Stores or Lifeway Christian Stores. Quotations marked NKJV are from the *New King
James Version.* Copyright © 1979, 1980, 1982.
Thomas Nelson, Inc., Publishers. Reprinted
with permission. Quotations marked NRSV
are from the *New Revised Standard Version
of the Bible,* copyright © 1989 by the Division

(Continued on page iv)

CONTENTS

Dedicated to
*Doris Lorraine
Steenland McLaren,*
National Merit Scholar,
on her graduation from
Martin Luther King Magnet High School
for Health Sciences and Engineering
Nashville, Tennessee
May 1997.
May you study to show yourself approved unto God
as you have studied to show yourself approved unto men
(2 Timothy 2:15).

(Acknowledgments continued from page ii)

of Christian Education of the National Council of the Churches of Christ in the United States of America. Used by permission. All rights reserved. Quotations marked Montgomery or Centenary are from *The New Testament in Modern English,* Centenary Translation by Helen Barrett Montgomery. Copyright © 1924 by Judson Press. Used by permission of Judson Press. Quotations marked REB are from *The Revised English Bible.* Copyright © Oxford University Press and Cambridge University Press, 1989. Reprinted by permission. Quotations marked RSV are from the *Revised Standard Version of the Bible,* copyright 1946, 1952, © 1971, 1973. Quotations marked Rotherham are from *The Emphasized New Testament,* by Joseph Bryant Rotherham, copyright © 1897, 1916 The Standard Publishing Company, Cincinnati. Kregal Publications. Quotations marked *Tanakh* are from *Tanakh: A New Translation of the Holy Scriptures according to the Traditional Hebrew Text,* copyright © 1985 The Jewish Publication Society. Quotations marked TEV or GNB are from the *Good News Bible,* the Bible in Today's Modern English Version. Old Testament: Copyright © American Bible Society 1976; New Testament: Copyright © American Bible Society 1966, 1971, 1976. Used by permission. This translation is available in a Holman Bible and can be ordered through Baptist Book Stores or Lifeway Christian Stores. Quotations marked Weymouth are from *Weymouth's New Testament In Modern Speech.* Copyright © 1902, 1909, 1912 Harper and Row, Publishers, Inc. Quotations marked Williams are from the *Williams New Testament in the Language of the People,* by Charles B. Williams. Copyright © 1937, 1966, 1986 by Holman Bible Publishers.

STUDY THEME: FACING LIFE HEAD-ON: DEVELOPING SPIRITUAL DISCIPLINES TO FACE PERSONAL CRISES AND SOCIAL ISSUES

UNIT I: *Basic Spiritual Disciplines*

June 1

PRAYER

Basic Passage: Psalm 86
Focal Passage: Psalm 86:1-17

INTRODUCTION

1. Christians are not obscurantists. We should not be like the proverbial ostrich and hide our heads in the ground. We are to face life head-on. Today begins a 14-week, three-unit study theme designed to help believers face head-on personal life crises and some of the issues confronting our society.

2. But before we can face life and its issues and crises head-on, we need to develop some basic spiritual disciplines for doing so. Thus this first unit focuses on five basic disciplines essential for spiritual growth: prayer, Bible study, personal worship, giving, and witnessing. Selected passages from the Book of Psalms provide the biblical bases for the lessons in this unit.

3. The Central Bible Truth of this lesson is that prayer involves humbly approaching God, confident that He accepts our praise and meets our needs according to His character.

4. The purpose of this lesson is to help you identify ways you will seek to improve the quality and depth of your prayers.

5. This lesson seeks to answer the question, How can I strengthen my prayer life?

I. SOME PRELIMINARY CONSIDERATIONS

1. The Book of Psalms

The Hebrew title for the Book of Psalms is *tehillim,* "songs of praise." This title reminds us that the poems we call psalms are songs–and songs are intended to be sung.

The Psalter was the hymnbook of the Second Temple. Most of the psalms in the Psalter, however, are older than the exilic and post-exilic periods of Israel's history. In fact, at least 73 psalms are attributed to David, the great song-writer king of Israel.

As we have it today, the Book of Psalms is divided into five books: Book I contains Psalms 1–41; Book II contains Psalms 42–72; Book III contains Psalms 73–89; Book IV contains Psalms 90–106; Book V contains Psalms 107–150. Some scholars believe this fivefold division is an attempt to imitate the five books of the Torah (Genesis–Deuteronomy).

As hymns, the psalms gave expression to the religious beliefs and heritage of Israel. Like our hymns today, the psalms mirror the spiritual experiences of the human soul in general–not merely record the personal religious experiences of the individual Hebrew poets.

Different ways to classify psalms have been proposed by scholars. Some scholars classify the psalms by their use in the temple (hymns of praise, prayers of thanksgiving, prayers of petition, etc.). Other scholars classify them by their subjects or content (hymns of adoration, psalms of thanksgiving, historical psalms, penitential psalms, imprecatory psalms, messianic psalms, etc.). Still other scholars classify them by their literary types or forms (laments, hymns, songs of thanksgiving, enthronement psalms, royal psalms, liturgical psalms, wisdom psalms, etc.).

In studying Hebrew poetry, it is important to realize their poetry bears little resemblance to what we mean by the term. In Hebrew poetry, rhyme did not exist, and it is more accurate to speak of rhythm than metre. Two distinctive characteristics of

Hebrew poetry, however, are helpful to understand in seeking to interpret it: the use of alphabetic devises and parallelism. Nine psalms use acrostic structures of one sort or another: 9; 10; 25; 34; 37; 111; 112; 119; and 145.

Parallelism is the distinctive feature of Hebrew poetry. Parallelism means that one line of poetry corresponds in some way with the next line of poetry. Scholars have identified several different types of parallelism. One type is called *constructive* or *synthetical parallelism.* In constructive parallelism one line of poetry serves as the basis upon which the next line of poetry builds. Psalm 19:7-10 provides a clear example of constructive parallelism. In *synonymous parallelism* the next line of poetry is the repetition of the same thought as in the previous line, only in different words. Every verse of Psalm 114 is written in synonymous parallelism. In *contrasted* or *antithetical parallelism* the statement in one line of poetry is affirmed in the next line of poetry by stating its opposite. Psalm 1:6 is a good example of antithetical parallelism. These types of parallelism are found throughout the poetry of the Psalter and are seen most clearly in Bibles that print the psalms in poetic lines rather than in prose form.

The Psalter occupied a large place in the life and teaching of our Lord. It was the prayer book for the synagogue and the hymnbook for the temple festivals. He used it in His teaching and quoted from it when tempted. He sang the Hallel from it with His disciples after the last supper, and He died with the words of a psalm on His lips.

For most of Christian history the church has sung the psalms and modeled its hymns after those contained in it. Believers have used the psalms as a devotional guide and found comfort in the words of the Psalter in times of crises.

2. The Nature of Prayer

In the Christian understanding, *prayer* is a speaking to or communication with God on the part of a believer or a believing people. As such, prayer can take many forms: praise, petition, intercession, confession, thanksgiving. Christians pray to God because He is a personal God who hears, cares, and is able to answer prayers. He desires that we pray to Him. Our prayers express what we believe about God, and they affect the personal relationship between God and us. A regular prayer life is essential to a Christian's growth in Christ.

II. FOCAL PASSAGE EXAMINED (Ps. 86:1-17)

Psalm 86 is the only psalm in the third book of the Psalter that is associated with David. It is an individual lament dominated by the imperative mode of prayer. In fact, only a few psalms have as many imperative petitions as this psalm–there are 14 of them. The lament and complaint are contained in the supplications in verses 1-7 and in verses 14-17. These two sections form a frame around verses 8-13, which contain the positive core of the psalm. In this positive core of the psalm the language changes from that of a lament into a hymn of praise in verses 8-10, followed by a request to be taught by the Lord in verse 11 and a vow of thanksgiving in verses 12-13 (see Marvin Tate, "Psalms 51–100," in the *Word Biblical Commentary,* vol. 20 [Dallas: Word Books, 1990], 377, 384).

1. Submission (Ps. 86:1-4)

The psalmist referred to himself no less than 35 times in this psalm. The occurrences of the first person personal pronoun are all supplications. Here we see the psalmist in prayer, speaking to God. He began by indicating his submission to God.

Verses 1-4: **Bow down thine ear, O Lord, hear me: for I am poor and needy. Preserve my soul; for I am holy: O thou my God, save thy servant that trusteth in thee. Be merciful unto me, O Lord: for I cry unto thee daily. Rejoice the soul of thy servant: for unto thee, O Lord, do I lift up my soul.**

Each of the psalmist's four petitions in verses 1-4 are based on a reason. Following the petition the reason is indicated by the word **for:** (1) **hear me . . . for I am poor and needy;** (2) **preserve my soul . . . for I am holy;** (3) **be merciful unto me . . . for I cry unto thee daily;** (4) **rejoice the soul of thy servant . . . for unto thee, O Lord, do I lift up my soul.**

First, the psalmist asked God to **bow down thine ear . . . hear me** or "hear and answer me." Notice that he addressed God as **O Lord.** The word **Lord,** printed in small capital letters in the *King James Version,* is the word for Jehovah or *Yahweh,* the covenant God of Israel. *Yahweh* (the LORD) is used four times in this psalm (vv. 1,6,11,17); *Adonai* (Lord) is used seven times (vv. 3,4,5,8,9,12,15); *Elohim* (God) is used five times (vv. 2,8,10,12,14; v. 8, however, refers to false gods); and *El* (God) is used once (v. 15).

In this first petition the psalmist laid before the Lord his condition: **I am poor and needy.** The Hebrew word for **poor** (*ani*) does not refer to economic poverty. The Hebrew word could be rendered "afflicted" (NASB) or "oppressed" (REB). The psalmist's cry to the Lord had its basis in distress and oppression. This should remind us that need and a sense for divine help can drive someone to cry out to God. However, in the Psalms **poor and needy** is a stylized idiom used to identify the godly person (35:10; 37:14; 40:17; 70:5; 109:16,22). Possibly the pair of words are not to be distinguished but taken together as a single description–a hendiadys [hen-DI-uh-duhs] construction in which the two adjectives coordinated by **and** form a single description rather than a double description: "I am the one who is afflicted with need." (The word *hendiadys* comes from the Greek term meaning "one through two.")

In the second petition, David asked God to **preserve my soul. Soul** (*nephesh*) here signifies the whole of one's life and being, not just a spiritual or nonmaterial component of the person. The *New International Version* correctly renders the petition "guard my life." One of David's named reasons was **for I**

am holy (*hasid*). This expression, while unique to here in the Hebrew Psalter, is not the self-righteous boast it may sound like in the *King James Version* rendering. The expression means "I am devoted to you" (NIV, NRSV), "I am faithful" (REB), or "I am a godly man" (NASB). And because David emphatically could declare, **O thou my God,** or better, "You are my God" (NIV), he could ask God to **save thy servant that trusteth in thee.** Here David named his second reason for this petition, using the word **servant** (*'ebed*) for the first time in these verses as a further demonstration of his commitment and relationship to the Lord. The word refers to a bondman. David, the loyal servant, was conscious that he was addressing his petition to a great overlord. **Trusteth** is an active participle. David continued to trust in the Lord and was waiting for His gracious response. David submitted himself fully to the protection of God.

In the third petition David asked God to **be merciful** to him and declared that he prayed to God **daily. Be merciful unto me** literally is "favor me." The Hebrew word was used of a superior bending or stooping in kindness to help an inferior. **Daily** literally is "all the day" or "all day long" (NIV).

David's fourth petition is a bold one. Using the word *sameah,* joyful or merry, David implored God, **Rejoice the soul of thy servant.** We would say "Gladden the soul" (NRSV), "Gladden the heart," "Fill your servant's heart with joy" (REB), or "Make my heart glad!" (CEV). David's basis for this was **for unto thee, O Lord, do I lift up my soul.** The word **soul** (*nephesh*) in verse 4b is the same Hebrew word as in verses 2, 13, and 14, where it means "life," but the *New International Version* leaves it translated **soul** here in verse 4b since it is in the context of David's lifting up his soul to God in prayer. It also is the same word as in verse 4a in the expression "gladden" or **rejoice the soul of thy servant.**

David began his prayer by admitting his need for God. He acknowledged his relationship and commitment to God and his need for God to give him mercy and joy.

Recognizing our need for God and submitting to His lordship in our lives are the first steps to seeing God answer our prayers and work on our behalf.

2. Confidence (Ps. 86:5-7)

The psalmist had confidence in the Lord because he knew the nature of his God.

Verses 5-7: **For thou, Lord, art good, and ready to forgive; and plenteous in mercy unto all them that call upon thee. Give ear, O Lord, unto my prayer; and attend to the voice of my supplications. In the day of my trouble I will call upon thee: for thou wilt answer me.**

Verse 6 is an example of synonymous parallelism where the same thought is repeated in different words. The phrase **Give ear, O Lord, unto my prayer** means the same thing as **attend to the voice of my supplications. Give ear** and **attend** mean "hear" (NIV) and "listen" (NIV), and **prayers** are the same as **supplications.**

David did not specify the exact nature of his afflictions, and the phrase **the day of my trouble** is a stylized expression in the Psalms (20:1; 50:15; 77:2). But in verse 5 David named three reasons he had confidence God would hear and **answer** his prayers: (1) God is **good;** (2) God is **ready to forgive;** and (3) God is **plenteous in mercy unto all them that call upon** Him.

First, the psalmist knew God is **good.** The Hebrew word is *tob.* It is the same goodness of God that David referred to in Psalm 23:6. The Hebrew word was used to describe the purity and high quality of things that were of superior character and worth. The word also was used of moral goodness. God is called **good** in 1 Chronicles 16:34 and in Psalm 145:9. In both cases His mercy also is mentioned. Of course, we learned this important theological truth early in our lives when we were taught the little blessing for our food: "God is great. God is good. Now let us thank Him for our food."

Second, the psalmist knew God is "forgiving" (NIV). The Hebrew word is *sallah*. This is the only time this adjective is used
in the Old Testament. Hence, it is called a *hapax legomenon*
[hah-pahks luh-GOHM-uh-non]. The verb form of the word,
however, is fairly common—but it always has God or the action of
God as its subject. The psalmist knew it is God's nature to be
ready to forgive.

Third, the psalmist knew God is **plenteous in mercy.** The
Hebrew word translated **mercy** is *hesed*. This word has no exact
English equivalent. It refers to mercy, kindness, love, goodness,
and favor all rolled up into one. The *New International Version*
has "abounding in love." "Lovingkindness" and "merciful love"
are good suggestions. In the Psalms, the **mercy** (*hesed*) of God
is presented as: (1) abundant or plenteous (5:7; 69:13; 103:8;
106:7,45); (2) great in extent (57:10; 103:11; 145:8); and (3) everlasting (100:5; 106:1; 107:1; 118:1,2,3,4,29; 136:1-26). The
psalmist knew it is God's nature to be rich in merciful love **unto
all them that call upon thee.**

As believers, we too can pray to God in faith and confidence,
knowing He will hear and respond to our prayers, not because of
our ability to believe more but because of His character and person. The God to whom we pray is a good, forgiving, and loving
God. That should give us all the confidence in the world to come
to Him in prayer daily.

3. Praise (Ps. 86:8-13)

Next, David praised God. Praise is an appropriate part of
prayer because it gives us the right perspective. Through praise
we acknowledge the nature and character of the One to whom
we are praying. Praise should be a significant part of our
prayers because praising God forces us to focus on God, the One
who answers our prayers, rather than merely on our needs and
problems. A right perspective seeks God's glory above our own
personal satisfaction.

When David praised God, his praise was not random. He looked to the past (v. 8), to the prospects of the future (v. 9), and to the present (v. 10). He made comparisons in the realms of heaven (v. 8a), nature (v. 8b), humankind (v. 9), and history (v. 10).

Verses 8-10: **Among the gods there is none like unto thee, O Lord; neither are there any works like unto thy works. All nations whom thou hast made shall come and worship before thee, O Lord; and shall glorify thy name. For thou art great, and doest wondrous things: thou art God alone.**

David's look to the past in verse 8 took him all the way back to heaven and to the **works** of God in creation. The reference to **the gods** should not be taken as an affirmation of the existence of others gods, or polytheism; for David clearly indicated his monotheism in verse 10, declaring **thou art God alone.** Most Bible students understand the reference to **the gods** as a rhetorical expression similar to Paul's in 1 Corinthians 8:5-6. Some scholars, however, believe David was referring to heavenly beings or angels (Derek Kidner, *Psalms 73–150,* in the Tyndale Old Testament Commentaries [London: Inter-Varsity Press, 1975], 312). **Thy works** here refers to the things God made, rather than the "deeds" (NIV) God did (which come in v. 10a).

David's look to the prospects of the future in verse 9 took him to a world founded on the **worship** of God. The prospect of world-wide homage, **all nations . . . shall come and worship before thee, O Lord; and shall glorify thy name,** is strong in David's writings (see especially Ps. 22:27-31). The logic for this universal homage is brought out in the words **whom thou hast made.**

David's look to the present in verse 10 caused him to see a world filled with the **wondrous things** of God around him. The term **wondrous things** is used frequently in the Psalms to refer to God's miracles of salvation (see 9:1; 78:4,11,32). And **thou art great** takes us back to the deep theological truth in the first half of that little children's blessing, "God is great. God is good."

Verse 11: **Teach me thy way, O Lord; I will walk in thy truth: unite my heart to fear thy name.**

With verses 11-13 David turned to himself. Indeed, verse 11 is the very heart or core of this psalm. It is a prayer within a prayer. "The incomparable God, the Worker of Wonders, is implored to teach the supplicant His, Yahweh's, **way,** so that the supplicant may walk in it with single-hearted obedience. This is followed by the prayer: 'Unite my heart to fear your name'" (Tate, "Psalms 51–100," 384). This is a prayer that involves forming the right habits and then making the right moves.

David named three important qualities in his prayer in verse 11. First, he asked for understanding of God's **way** in the world: **Teach me thy way, O Lord.** David's deepest need, as is ours, was for understanding. In times of trouble, those who are wise seek to learn God's ways in the world. Our complaints and supplications need to be informed by insight into the nature of life in God's creation and the manner of God's action.

Second, David declared, **I will walk in thy truth.** David was committed to a lifestyle that reflected God's truth. Oh, how we contemporary Christians need to learn a lesson here! Without a commitment to live faithfully according to God's truth, our prayers and petitions to God, no matter how often we repeat them, mean little. Our petitions to God will gain power only when we are willing to live lives of trust in and faithfulness to Him.

Third, David prayed, **Unite my heart to fear thy name.** This is a petition for single-hearted devotion to God. The *New International Version* reads, "Give me an undivided heart." The word **unite** is *yached,* meaning "to make one." David wanted to be united in purpose with God. David knew, as James later wrote, that the double-minded person will not receive anything he or she asks from the Lord (Jas. 1:7-8). **Heart** refers to the inner volitional self, to the core of one's being where the will and behavior are shaped.

Modern psychology talks about the disintegrated state of the human being. Psychological wholeness, psychologists claim, results from becoming a fully integrated person. Two thousand years before modern psychology David knew about the disintegrated state of the human being. But "his concern is not with unifying his personality for its own sake; the lines meet at a point beyond himself, the fear of the Lord" (Kidner, *Psalms 73–150*, 313). J. J. Stewart Perowne paraphrased David's prayer: "Suffer it [my heart] no more to scatter itself upon a multiplicity of objects, to be drawn hither and thither by a thousand aims, but to turn all its powers, all its affections in one direction, collect them in one focus, make them all one in Thee" (*The Book of Psalms*, vol. II [Grand Rapids: Zondervan Publishing House, 1966 reprint], 130).

Verses 12-13: **I will praise thee, O Lord my God, with all my heart: and I will glorify thy name for evermore. For great is thy mercy toward me: and thou hast delivered my soul from the lowest hell.**

David did not wait passively for the spiritual maturity for which he prayed in verse 11 before he began to praise the **Lord** (*adonai*) his **God** (*elohim*). David declared he would **praise** and **glorify** God with **all my heart** and **for evermore.** As in verse 5, the word translated **mercy** is *hesed*–"lovingkindness." As before, the *New International Version* uses "love." The phrase **thou hast delivered my soul from the lowest hell** is difficult, first, because it is possible to understand this as either past or future, and, second, because it could be a sober reference to the state after death or it could be a figurative expression for a serious crisis or adversity–"the very brink of death" (as in 88:6). **From the lowest hell** literally is "from Sheol," the unseen world beneath. The *New International Version* renders the phrase, "you have delivered me from the depths of the grave." The word **soul** (*nephesh*) is the same word as in verses 2, 4, and 14, but it does not help in deciding the meaning of the phrase because *nephesh* can refer to one's "life" or to the nonmaterial part of the human constitution that survives death. In this psalm, the *King James Version* consistently translates it "soul";

the *New International Version* uses "life" in verses 2 and 14, "soul" in verse 4, and "me" in verse 13. Perhaps the best we can say here is that David praised God for His deliverance, whether temporal or eternal.

Praise should be part of our daily prayer time. David praised God for His holiness and uniqueness. David praised God for what He had made and for what He had done. David praised God for His love and deliverance. What do you praise God for during your daily prayer time?

4. Petition (Ps. 86:14-17)

In verses 14-17 David returned to his supplication, his complaint. In contrast to verses 1-7 where David's complaint was general, here he is specific—there was an immediate threat.

Verses 14-17: O God, the proud are risen against me, and the assemblies of violent men have sought after my soul; and have not set thee before them. But thou, O Lord, art a God full of compassion, and gracious, long-suffering, and plenteous in mercy and truth. O turn unto me, and have mercy upon me; give thy strength unto thy servant, and save the son of thine handmaid. Show me a token for good; that they which hate me may see it, and be ashamed: because thou, Lord, hast holpen me, and comforted me.

The proud who had **risen against** David were "arrogant" (NIV) people. **The assemblies of violent men** who **sought after** his **soul** ("life," NIV) are likened to a gang or pack of animals (see 68:30 where the same word is used). They were "a band of ruthless men" (NIV). No reason is given for their actions. The verb in **are risen against me** may suggest a legal offense with which David was charged (as in 27:12) or it may mean "risen up to attack," putting David's life in physical danger (as in 27:3). The expressions, however, may be merely a stylized way of personifying adversity (see Ps. 54:3).

In contrast, **but thou, O Lord,** God is **full of compassion, gracious, long-suffering,** and **plenteous in mercy and truth.** David based this view of God on Scripture. Verse 15 is a word-for-word quotation of Exodus 34:6b. **Full of compassion** is the Hebrew word *rahum.* This adjective, which means "compassionate" or "merciful," is used only of God in the Old Testament. **Gracious** is the Hebrew word *hannun.* It is used 13 times in the Old Testament, 11 of which are in combination with *rahum* (compassionate, merciful), and always in reference to God. This adjective describes the gracious acts of the Lord. The most important occurrence of the word is in Exodus 34:6 in conjunction with the great proclamation of the name of God to Moses on Mount Sinai. **Long-suffering** is two words in the Hebrew, "long" and "to anger." The *New International Version*'s "slow to anger" is a good translation. **Plenteous in mercy** is the important Hebrew word *hesed* ("loving kindness," NASB; "steadfast love," NRSV) again. The *New International Version* has "abounding in love," as in verse 5. **Truth** is the Hebrew word *emet.* The word means "truth" or "verity," but it carries the underlying sense of "dependability" or "certainty." Hence, the *New International Version*'s rendering "faithfulness" (also the NRSV). The word always is used in contexts that relate to God—His person, His words, His revelation, His salvation, His peace. All truth is related to God. Since this word often is coupled with *hesed* ("mercy," KJV; "love," NIV), it is possible these two words are here used as a hendiadys (where two words are used to describe one concept) meaning "true/faithful loyal-love."

David also petitioned God for **strength** and for a "sign" (NIV) or **a token for good.** David's plea for a sign literally reads "with me a sign for goodness." He asked God for a sign for his welfare or a sign that all would be well. The *New Revised Standard Version* reads "show me a sign of your favor." David wanted those who opposed him to see this sign and be put to shame.

David again identified himself as **thy servant** and asked God to **save** him (see v. 2). However, this time David also identified

himself as **the son of thine handmaid.** This "expression denotes a person who belongs to the household by birth, not an
outsider or slave purchased by the master of the household"
(Tate, "Psalms 51–100," 383).

David had confidence in God's future help because the Lord
helped him in the past: **thou . . . hast holpen me, and comforted me. Holpen** means "helped" (NIV). The Hebrew word
azar most often was used of military assistance or divine assistance of a military nature. In the Psalms the Lord is seen as the
helper of the poor (72:12) and the fatherless (10:14). He is a
helper at times of affliction (28:7), oppression from others (54:4),
and great personal distress (86:17). God's hand and His laws were
sources of divine help to the psalmist (119:173,175). **Comforted
me** is the Hebrew word *naham.* This is the same word David
used in Psalm 23:4 when he wrote, "Thy rod and thy staff they
comfort me." It is the same word Isaiah used in opening his message to the exiles, *"nahamu nahamu 'ammi"* or "comfort ye, comfort ye my people, saith your God" (Isa. 40:1). While some comfort
may be gained from other human beings (Isa. 66:13), God is the
source of true comfort for His people (Pss. 71:21; 86:17; 119:82).

Interestingly, these final verses do not reveal any abatement
of the pressure or any sign of an answer from God. We are left
with an as yet unanswered prayer. But even though we do not
see an answer, we do see God. Four times over David made direct affirmations about God. In verse 5 he said, **Thou, Lord,
art good, and ready to forgive.** In verse 10 he said, **Thou art
great** and **thou art God alone.** In verse 15 he said, **Thou, O
Lord, art . . . full of compassion, and gracious.** In verse 17
he said, **Thou, Lord, hast holpen me, and comforted me.**
And this is indeed why prayer is so important–it puts us in
touch with God. Because God is who He is, we can bring our specific needs and petitions before Him, pray for His help, and trust
Him to do what is best. And having done so, we can rest in the
comfort He gives–even if we can't see His answer yet.

June 8

BIBLE STUDY

Basic Passage: Psalm 119
Focal Passages: Psalm 119:10-11,16,18,33-37,
　　　　　　　　57-60,89,137-138

INTRODUCTION

1. The great missionary David Livingstone once declared, "All that I am I owe to Jesus Christ revealed to me in His divine Book" (quoted in Virginia Ely, *I Quote* [Westwood, N.J.: Fleming H. Revell Co., 1947], 29).

2. Victorious Christians through the ages have drunk from the Bible's everflowing stream and fed upon its manna, which is fresh for every day and experience of life. The psalmist of old found this to be the case.

3. The Central Bible Truth of this lesson is that the Bible is God's trustworthy Word that believers are to study and obey.

4. The purpose of this lesson is to help you commit to the spiritual discipline of Bible study in order to know God and obey Him.

5. This lesson seeks to answer the question, How can I make the Bible a more significant part of my life?

I.   SOME PRELIMINARY CONSIDERATIONS

1. The Background

Psalm 119 is an alphabetic acrostic based on the 22 letters of the Hebrew alphabet. Each alphabetic section consists of eight verses, with each verse in a given section beginning with the same letter of the Hebrew alphabet. For instance, the first eight verses are the *aleph* or "a" section. The opening word of each

verse begins with this letter. The other 21 sections of eight
verses each follow the rest of the Hebrew alphabet in succession.
This explains the length of the psalm, 176 verses, the longest in
the Psalter. This also explains why the psalm is printed in 22
strophes in some Bibles, with a Hebrew letter over each strophe.

We do not know who wrote Psalm 119, but it probably was
written in the post-exilic era. The psalm's length indicates it is
unlikely it was used in public worship. Most likely Psalm 119
was used in private study and meditation.

2. Words About the Word

The psalmist used eight words to describe God's Word in Psalm
119. These words are repeated over and over throughout the
psalm. "Law" (*torah*) occurs 25 times. "Word" (*dabar*) occurs 24
times. "Laws" (*mispatim*) occurs 23 times. "Statute" or "statutes"
(*edut* or *edot*) occurs 23 times. "Command" or "commands" (*mis-
wah* or *miswot*) occurs 22 times. "Decrees" (*huqqim*) occurs 21
times. "Precepts" (*piqqudim*) occurs 21 times. And "word" or
"promise" (*'imrah*) occurs 19 times. Together these words provide
a good understanding and definition of God's Word. Thus it is evi-
dent that the purpose of the psalm is to show God's Word as a
treasure of instruction, inspiration, and guidance.

II.   FOCAL PASSAGES EXAMINED
   (Ps. 119:10-11,16,18,33-37,57-60,89,137-138)

As one begins this study, he or she should reverently hold in
his or her hand the Bible, for the theme of Psalm 119 is God's
Word. To Christians that Word is the Old and New Testaments.
The Bible is not *a book* but *the Book*. Books are the treasure-
houses of the minds of their authors. *The Book* is the treasurehouse of the mind of God. It is not God, as other books are not
their authors. But the Bible is God's written revelation of Himself. It is His written Word.

Someone has called Psalm 119 "The ABC's of the Law." In a sense this is true, for in it one finds the basic elements of God's law. Seen in another way, it is a meditation upon God's law from A to Z. The alphabetic acrostic form is the author's way of expressing the comprehensive nature of God's law. In poetic fashion, he said God's revelation contains all that one needs to know.

To this must be added what Willem VanGemeren said of this beautiful psalm: "This is a psalm, not only of law, but of love, not only of statute, but of spiritual strength, not only of devotion to precept, but of loyalty to the way of the Lord. The beauty in this psalm resounds from the relationship of the psalmist and his God" ("Psalms," in *The Expositor's Bible Commentary,* vol. 5 [Grand Rapids: Zondervan Publishing House, 1991], 736-737).

1. Make Bible Study a Priority (Ps. 119:10-11,16)

These verses come from the second or *Beth* strophe (vv. 9-16), named after the second letter of the Hebrew alphabet.

Verses 10-11: With my whole heart have I sought thee: O let me not wander from thy commandments. Thy word have I hid in mine heart, that I might not sin against thee.

Verse 16: I will delight myself in thy statutes: I will not forget thy word.

Why did the psalmist seek to make studying God's Word a priority in his life? For its own sake? No! Merely to acquire more information? No, again. To show off his learning? Not a bit.

The psalmist knew he was not sufficient in-and-of-himself to live the kind of life God required of him. The purpose for which he desired to accumulate a store of divine precepts was so that they might be a defense against sin within him. In verse 9 the psalmist raised the issue of moral and spiritual cleansing: "Wherewithal shall a young man cleanse his way?" Or, "How can a young man keep his way pure?" (NIV). The answer is to heed and obey God's Word.

That he might not **wander** from God's **commandments** (*miswot*) or **sin against** God, the psalmist had hidden away in his **heart** what God had said. The **word** the psalmist said he had hidden in his heart is the word of promise (*'imrah*). The heart that stores up Scripture has its judgment informed by God. What at first might look like a good opportunity or an open door circumstantially actually might be a closed door scripturally. So the psalmist pledged, **I will not forget thy word.** There is little point in reading or studying the Bible if you immediately forget what it says. The psalmist might not always have a Bible in hand, but he would have its precepts in his heart.

This suggests the importance of leading children to memorize Scripture. During their formative years their minds are like sponges, soaking up knowledge. In this vital period they should be encouraged and guided in hiding God's Word in their minds and hearts. It will serve them well later on. And what is true for children is true for adults too.

But hiding God's Word in our hearts should not be limited to memorizing individual verses or even whole chapters of the Bible. Hiding God's Word in our hearts extends to living a holy life of devotion to God. The words in verse 10, **let me not wander from thy commandments,** refer to deliberate sin, not unconscious straying. Bible study should be a priority for those who have committed to live their lives by the moral teachings found in God's Word. Bible study should be a priority because we desire to govern our lives by the Lord's revealed standards.

These verses demonstrate that we must begin with an inner decision and commitment. The psalmist's decision involved his **whole heart.** In his **heart** he hid God's Word. In his inner being he experienced **delight.** In his memory he would not **forget** God's Word.

The psalmist made Bible study a priority because of his sincere love for God. The psalmist said, **With my whole heart have I sought thee.** Wholehearted commitment is the key. Anyone who tries to follow God's moral standards halfheartedly will fail. Halfhearted commitment is the plague of modern Christianity–and of many Southern Baptist churches. God calls for total commitment from His people. We are like the chicken in the story of the chicken and the pig that were asked to make a donation to a church's ham-and-egg breakfast. The chicken told the pig she thought it was a good idea–she'd provide the eggs. But the pig declined, replying, "No way! For you, it would be an inconvenience; for me, it would be total commitment!"

Why should Bible study be a priority? In this strophe the psalmist indicated three reasons. First, because God's Word has a cleansing effect: it will assist you in cleansing your ways (v. 9). Second, because God's Word has a controlling effect: it will keep you from wandering from God's commandments (v. 10). Third, because God's Word has a correcting effect: hiding God's Word in your heart will keep you from sinning against God (vv. 11-12).

2. Read and Study the Bible Prayerfully (Ps. 119:18,33-37)

In these verses the psalmist asked God both to *open his eyes* and to *close his eyes*. Thereby he reminded us that through Bible study we are to see some things and to turn away from other things.

Verse 18: **Open thou mine eyes, that I may behold wondrous things out of thy law.**

Open thou mine eyes is a prayer for spiritual insight. Verse 18, which belongs to the *gimel* strophe, reminds us we should begin our daily devotions or Bible study with a prayer for God to open our eyes to the spiritual truth in His Word. It reminds us there are depths to God's Word that cannot be fathomed without divine aid. It further reminds us that spiritual things must be spiritually received and that we do not naturally understand the things of God (1 Cor. 2:14). When God opens our eyes to His truth, what was plain–or perhaps even dull–to us suddenly becomes **wondrous things out of thy law** (*torah*).

Clara H. Scott grasped the meaning of this statement and provided the church a wonderful hymn-prayer:

> Open my eyes, that I may see
>> Glimpses of truth Thou hast for me;
> Place in my hands the wonderful key
>> That shall unclasp and set me free:
> Silently now I wait for Thee,
>> Ready, my God, Thy will to see;
> Open my eyes, illumine me, Spirit divine!

("Open My Eyes, That I May See," No. 502, *The Baptist Hymnal,* 1991.)

The next verses of our study, verses 33-37, are from the *he* strophe (vv. 33-40). Each of the verses begins with the Hebrew causative *he,* thus lending itself naturally to a series of prayers related to God's working in the psalmist's life. The strophe contains a number of causative imperatives: **teach me** (v. 33), **give me** (v. 34), **make me** (v. 35), **incline my heart** (v. 36), **turn away mine eyes** (v. 37), **stablish thy word** (v. 38), **turn away my reproach** (v. 39).

Verses 33-37: **Teach me, O Lord, the way of thy statutes; and I shall keep it unto the end. Give me understanding, and I shall keep thy law; yea, I shall observe it with my whole heart. Make me to go in the path of thy commandments; for therein do I delight. Incline my heart unto thy testimonies, and not to covetousness. Turn away mine eyes from beholding vanity; and quicken thou me in thy way.**

Teach me (*torehni*) is the Hebrew verb from which the word *torah* comes. Notice the psalmist did not merely pray, "Teach me thy statutes," but **Teach me . . . the way of thy statutes.** He asked for more than just knowledge of God's Word; he asked for a way of life based on God's Word.

I shall keep it unto the end may be translated "in keeping them I shall find my reward" (REB, NEB). This is because the Hebrew word for **unto the end** (*'eqeb*) is used in this psalm to mean "continually" or "always" (v. 44) and to mean "as a reward"

(v. 72; see also 19:11). Most modern translations (including the KJV and NIV) favor the former interpretation; most modern commentators favor the latter. The same debate between the commentators and the translations occurs over this word in verse 112.

Give me understanding reminds us there is a difference between knowledge and understanding. One can gain knowledge by reading and studying the Bible, but that does not mean one has understood and adopted into one's life the principles taught in the Bible.

Perhaps it seems contradictory for the psalmist to pray **make me to go in the path of thy commandments** and then to add **for therein do I delight.** Why should he have to be made to do something he delighted in doing? Because, like every believer, he was caught between the pull of his old nature and his new nature (see Rom. 7:22-23). In saying **make me to go in the path of thy commandments,** the psalmist pointed to God's Word as a **path** to be followed through the moral wilderness of this world.

The psalmist's petitions in verses 36-37 are in synonymous parallelism: **Incline my heart unto thy testimonies, and not to covetousness** and **Turn away mine eyes from beholding vanity.** The psalmist asked God to **incline my heart,** or "bend all my desires," because he knew there are distractions that keep us or beguile us from reading and studying God's Word. He knew the inclinations of his heart had to be touched by God. And he also knew a great deal of temptation comes to us through our **eyes.** Sinful things often have a great attraction for us. Like Eve we see and then desire (Gen. 3:6). The psalmist knew that in our own strength we will vacillate between the things of God and the attractions of the world.

In verses 36 and 37 the psalmist named two of these attractions. **Covetousness** refers to financial pursuits and profits—material gain. The *New International Version* has "selfish gain." The other named distraction is **vanity.** The word **vanity** (*saw*) refers to that which is hollow, valueless, worthless, or trivial. The *New International Version* has "worthless things." The psalmist prayed his eyes would be turned away from trivialities. In the Old Testament this word is part of the vocabulary for moral evil.

Clearly, the psalmist knew that one of the principles of spiritual victory is to look away. He also knew that in our own strength it is hard to take our eyes away from the attractive temptations around us. He knew he couldn't do much about all the vain temptations around him, so he did not ask God to remove the wickedness in the world but to cause him to **turn away mine eyes.**

Then the psalmist prayed, **Quicken thou me in thy way.** The words are rendered "preserve my life according to your word" in the *New International Version*. In this case, the *King James Version* follows the Hebrew Masoretic text's (the Hebrew text to which the vowels have been added to the words) **in thy way** more closely than the *New International Version* does with "according to your word."

This is one of the psalmist's nine prayers for quickening in this psalm (vv. 25,37,40,88,107,149,154,156,159). **Quicken** means "to be made alive." We need all the new life God has given to us to turn our eyes away from this world's vanities. The hymn writer knew what the psalmist meant when she wrote:

Turn your eyes upon Jesus, Look full in His wonderful face,
    And the things of earth will grow strangely dim
In the light of His glory and grace.

(Helen H. Lemmel, "Turn Your Eyes upon Jesus," No. 320, *The Baptist Hymnal,* 1991.)

3. Obey the Bible's Truths (Ps. 119:57-60)

When the psalmist considered his ways, he turned to God's Word and promised to obey God's commands without hesitation. These verses come from the *heth* strophe (vv. 57-64).

Verses 57-60: **Thou art my portion, O Lord: I have said that I would keep thy words. I entreated thy favor with my whole heart: be merciful unto me according to thy word. I thought on my ways, and turned my feet unto thy testimonies. I made haste, and delayed not to keep thy commandments.**

The words **Thou art my portion** are a formulaic expression that goes back to the early days of the levitical priesthood. When the Israelites conquered the land of Canaan and divided it among the 12 tribes, the tribe of Levi did not receive a portion of the land (Josh. 21). Instead, their portion was in the Lord Himself. It was upon Him they were to depend for their material support (Num. 18:20-21). **Portion** expresses the idea of a worthwhile inheritance. Leslie C. Allen ("Psalms 101–150," in the *Word Biblical Commentary,* vol. 21 [Waco: Word Books, 1983], 136) pointed out that the formula was used in complaint psalms as an expression of trust in the Lord (16:5; 73:26; 142:5). The *Good News Bible* translates it: "You are all I want, O Lord."

In verse 57 the psalmist pointed out an important biblical truth–the *person* of the Lord comes before the *precept* of the Lord. **Thou art my portion, O Lord: I have said that I would keep thy words.** It is because of who the Lord was to the psalmist that the psalmist pledged to **keep** or obey the words of the Lord. Jesus said the same thing for New Testament believers: "If ye love me, keep my commandments" (John 14:15).

In the phrase **I entreated thy favor,** the word **favor** literally is "face." The psalmist, as it were, had a face-to-face conversation with God. **Be merciful unto me** reminds us God is a God of mercy. **According to thy word** reminds us He has promised mercy to those who call upon Him.

John Phillips (*Exploring the Psalms,* vol. 2 [Neptune, N.J.: Loizeaux Brothers, 1988], 315-316) pointed out four important aspects of the psalmist's obedience in verse 59. First, the psalmist said, **I thought.** Here is *deliberation.* He stopped and thought. Second, the psalmist said, **I thought on my ways.**

He thought about where his life was taking him. He thought about the way he was living. In other words, he thought about his *destination*. Thinking about your ways and where they are taking you is the first sign of spiritual sanity. This was true of the prodigal son (Luke 15:17), and it is true of us today. Third, the psalmist said, **I . . . turned my feet.** Here was *determination*. This was the turning point in his life. He made a decision. Finally, he said, **I . . . turned . . . unto thy testimonies.** The psalmist did not turn to human wisdom, self-help philosophies, religious systems, or 12-step programs. He turned to God and His Word. Here is *discrimination*.

Further, the psalmist said he **delayed not.** The word **delayed** is the same word used of Lot when he lingered in Sodom, reluctant to leave the city. But there was no lingering hesitation on the psalmist's part: **I made haste, and delayed not.** By nature we are procrastinators. We have an inbred tendency to delay, to put off until tomorrow what we should do today. We have the attitude, "Mañana. Mañana." So too in the spiritual realm, we delay, stall, and postpone our obedience to God. Not so the psalmist. He believed in prompt obedience.

Those who seek to study the Bible effectively obey the truths of God's Word without hesitation or delay.

4. Recognize the Bible's Character
(Ps. 119:89,137-138)

The psalmist turned to God's Word because he recognized it as eternal, right, and trustworthy. Verse 89 belongs to the *lamedh* strophe (vv. 89-96).

Verse 89: **Forever, O Lord, thy word is settled in heaven.**

The fact that God's **word is settled in heaven** means "God's Word is lifted above all the changes wrought by time, above all the vicissitudes of life, above the temporality and transience of earth." The **word** is permanent because it is God's Word, and God is omniscient in His wisdom. The fact that God's **word is**

settled in heaven also means that "it is beyond the reach of man. No person, however clever, confident, or confused, will permanently change God's Word" (Phillips, *Exploring the Psalms,* vol. 2, 342-343). God's Word is far beyond the reach of its foes.

Voltaire (1694–1778), the French atheist and writer, held up a copy of the Bible and proclaimed, "In fifty years I'll have this book in the morgue." In fifty years Voltaire was in the morgue, and the Geneva Bible Society owned his house and used it to store Bibles!

The hymn writer Haldor Lillenas (1885-1959) put it well:

> The Bible stands like a rock undaunted,
>   'Mid the raging storms of time;
> Its pages burn with the truth eternal,
>   And they glow with a light sublime.
>
> The Bible stands like a mountain tow'ring
>   Far above the words of men;
> Its truth by none ever was refuted,
>   And destroy it they never can.
>
> The Bible stands and it will for ever,
>   When the world has passed away;
> By inspiration it has been given,
>   All its precepts I will obey.
>
> The Bible stands ev'ry test we give it,
>   For its author is divine;
> By grace alone I expect to live it,
>   And to prove it and make it mine.
>
> The Bible stands tho' the hills may tumble,
>   It will firmly stand when the earth shall crumble;
> I will plant my feet on its firm foundation,
>   For the Bible stands.

Verses 137-138: **Righteous art thou, O Lord, and upright are thy judgments. Thy testimonies that thou hast commanded are righteous and very faithful.**

These verses belong to the *tsadhe* strophe (vv. 137-144).

In verses 137-138 the psalmist affirmed that God is right in His character and right in His commands: **Righteous art thou, O Lord** and **Thy testimonies that thou hast commanded are righteous.** God does not make mistakes. It is impossible for Him to be wrong. Further, the psalmist knew God will never lead us astray in what He tells us. "Trust in the reliability of God's word is directly proportionate to one's trust in the Lord himself" (VanGemeren, "Psalms," 759).

Because the Lord is **righteous** (*saddiq*), His **judgments** (*mispatim*) or "laws" (NIV) and His **testimonies** (*'edot*) or "statutes" (NIV) are **righteous** (*sedeq*), **upright** (*yasar*), and **faithful** (*'emunah*) or "fully trustworthy" (NIV). They also are "pure" (*serupah*, v. 140; KJV) or "thoroughly tested" (NIV), "the truth" (*'emet,* v. 142; KJV) or "true" (NIV), and "everlasting" (*le'olam*, vv. 142,144; KJV and the NIV in v. 142) or "forever" (v. 144, NIV). The psalmist's conviction that the Lord and His Word are righteous and faithful evoked a response of great devotion and "zeal" from him (v. 139).

As believers we need to practice the spiritual discipline of Bible study because God's words are eternal, right, and trustworthy. When we do, we will discover our zeal for the Lord and the study of His Word will increase.

All of us can make the Bible a more significant part of our lives by making Bible study a priority, by reading and studying the Bible prayerfully, by obeying the Bible's truths, and by recognizing the Bible's character. Why not commit to spend some time with the Word each day? Why not start enjoying that daily heavenly manna today?

June 15

PERSONAL WORSHIP

Basic Passage: Psalm 145
Focal Passages: Psalm 145:1-5,8-12,17-19

INTRODUCTION

1. Some Christians think worship is only for Sundays. In fact, worship should be a daily event in the lives of believers.

2. Some Christians think of worship only as a corporate activity. In fact, Christians should practice both corporate worship and daily personal worship.

3. The Central Bible Truth of this lesson is that daily, personal worship is a vital part of a believer's relationship with God.

4. The purpose of this lesson is to help you identify steps you will take to establish or strengthen a daily time of worship.

5. This lesson seeks to answer the question, How can I strengthen my time of personal worship?

I. SOME PRELIMINARY CONSIDERATIONS

1. The Background

Psalm 145 is the last of nine alphabetical or acrostic psalms in the Psalter (Pss. 9; 10; 25; 34; 37; 111; 112; 119; 145). There are 22 letters in the Hebrew alphabet. Each verse of this psalm starts with one of the letters, with the exception of the Hebrew letter *nun,* which should come between verses 13 and 14. However, most of the ancient versions (including the Syriac and the Septuagint, the Greek translation of the Old Testament), a Dead Sea Scroll from Qumran (11Q Ps[a]), and one manuscript of the Hebrew Masoretic Text include the missing verse. Most modern versions, like the *New International Version,* include the missing verse as 13b (NRSV, CEV) or as 14a (NEB, REB). The *King James Version* and the *New American Standard Bible* do not include the addition.

Psalm 145 is also the last of the psalms that bears David's name. In fact, six of the nine alphabetic psalms bear David's name (Pss. 111; 112; 119 do not).

2. A Psalm of Worship

This is a psalm of pure worship. In Jewish liturgy Psalm 145 was used in the daily prayers. It was read twice in the morning and once in the evening. Thus Psalm 145 was part of worship day in and day out. The Talmud commends all who repeat this psalm three times a day, stating they have a share in the world to come (*Berakot* 4b). It is appropriate then that we consider this psalm in a lesson on the spiritual discipline of daily personal worship.

II. FOCAL PASSAGES EXAMINED
(Ps. 145:1-5,8-12,17-19)

The Hebrew title over this psalm is unique in the Psalter. This psalm is called a *tehillah*, a "praise" or "hymn." The plural form of this word, *tehillim*, is the Hebrew title for the entire Psalter. W. O. E. Oesterley said, "As a hymn of praise to God this psalm stands out as one of the most beautiful in the Psalter" (*The Psalms: Translated with Text-Critical and Exegetical Notes* [London: S. P. C. K., 1953], 575).

1. Worship Daily (Ps. 145:1-2)

Our English word *worship* means "worthship" and denotes the worthiness of one to receive honor in accordance with that worth. It is fitting then for worship to begin in adoration and praise.

Verses 1-2: **I will extol thee, my God, O king; and I will bless thy name forever and ever. Every day will I bless thee; and I will praise thy name forever and ever.**

The synonyms for praise in verses 1-2 set the tone for the psalm: **I will *extol* thee, I will *bless* thy name, every day will I *bless* thee,** and **I will *praise* thy name.** As always, the word **name** connotes God's character, the sum of all that God has disclosed about Himself.

The object of David's praise is **my God, O king.** From David's statement we see two reasons why he wanted to praise God. First and foremost, he had a personal relationship with Him. To David, God was **my God.** One cannot truly praise and worship God without a personal relationship with Him. God is not an abstract force or impersonal being, the great spirit of the universe.

The following story is told of Dr. H. A. Ironside, former pastor of Moody Church in Chicago, who was attending a large religious convention. A clergyman rose to give the invocation. He began his prayer with repetitious phrases like, "O Great Spirit. O eternal One. O Lord of the universe. O sovereign ruler of all things." On and on he went. Finally, Dr. Ironside was heard to mutter, "O just call Him *Father* and get on with it!" God may be all these other things by position, but the important thing is whether we have a personal relationship with Him.

The second reason David offered praise to God was because he had accepted God's rule over his life. To David, God was **king** of his life. David himself was a king—and a great king at that! Yet he acknowledged God's kingship over him. Jennie Hussey reminded us that this is where each of us must start as well:

> King of my life, I crown Thee now,
>   Thine shall the glory be;
> Lest I forget Thy thorn-crowned brow,
>   Lead me to Calvary.

("Lead Me to Calvary," No. 490, *The Baptist Hymnal,* 1991.)

Next, David indicated when he would worship God. In this he took both the immediate view and the long-term view. As a believer, David knew God's people will worship and praise Him for all eternity. So twice in these two verses he noted this, saying, **I will bless thy name forever and ever** and **I will praise thy name forever and ever.** But David didn't want to wait until eternity to begin to worship God. So he pledged, **Every day will I bless thee.** Our lives are made up of days. David determined that not a day would go by that he would not worship God. Do you worship God only on Sundays–a mere 52 (or less) days a year? David worshiped God 365 days a year–and so should we.

David's worship of God was worthy of Him and continuous. In making these statements the great singer and poet of Israel called on us to join him in this pledge. Will you worship God every day? Will you cultivate in your life the spiritual discipline of daily personal worship? If a busy king could do it, so can you!

2. Focus on God (Ps. 145:3-5,8-9)

The reason for David's commitment to daily personal worship lay in God–His greatness (vv. 3-5) and His goodness (vv. 8-9). Worship is about God. Therefore, it is important that we focus on God in our daily worship. This includes focusing both on what He has done and on who He is.

Verses 3-5: **Great is the Lord, and greatly to be praised; and his greatness is unsearchable. One generation shall praise thy works to another, and shall declare thy mighty acts. I will speak of the glorious honor of thy majesty, and of thy wondrous works.**

In David's personal worship, God's greatness involved His mystery, might, and majesty (vv. 3-5). David focused on the greatness of God in verse 3. He said that because **the Lord** is **great,** He is **greatly to be praised.** Then he noted that God's **greatness is unsearchable.** Herein lies the mystery of God. Six of ten uses of the noun **unsearchable** (*heqer*) in the Old Testament refer to the unsearchable nature of God (Job 5:9; 9:10; 36:26; Ps. 145:3; Isa. 40:28). In the Book of Job, Zophar asked, "Canst thou by searching find out God? canst thou find out the Almighty unto perfection?" (11:7). And in his speech, Elihu said, "Great things doeth he, which we cannot comprehend" (Job 37:5). For all of His self-revelation to us, we can never "fathom" (NIV) the depths of God's being. In Isaiah 55:8-9 God said, "For my thoughts are not your thoughts, neither are your ways my ways, saith the Lord. For as the heavens are higher than the earth, so are my ways higher than your ways, and my thoughts than your thoughts." This is the same point Paul made in Romans 11 when he wrote: "O the depth of the riches both of the wisdom and knowledge of God! how unsearchable are his judgments, and his ways past finding out" (v. 33; see also vv. 34-36). This is what theologians refer to as the infinity of God. God is not limited, nor is He limitable. We may know Him truly, but we will never comprehend Him fully. In the final analysis, God is inscrutable.

The **works** and **mighty acts** of God are something that **one generation** shall tell **to another.** David saw himself and other believers as part of a holy relay race in which one generation passes on to the next generation the story of God's mighty works (see Ps. 22:30-31). The process of transmission is by praising (v. 4a), declaring (v. 4b), and speaking (v. 5). This is one reason to support Christian education, Sunday Schools, and other Bible study efforts.

In verse 5 David noted the **majesty** of God. From speaking about what the believing community would do, David stated what he would do. According to the Hebrew manuscripts the *King James Version* followed, David began to state what he would do at the start of verse 5, saying, **I will speak of the glorious honor of thy majesty.** In the Hebrew text the words are piled up and literally read, "the glory of the splendor of the majesty." According to the Hebrew manuscripts the *New International Version* followed, however, David did not begin to state what he would do until the second half of verse 5, saying, "I will meditate on your wonderful works."

Verses 8-9: **The Lord is gracious, and full of compassion; slow to anger, and of great mercy. The Lord is good to all: and his tender mercies are over all his works.**

A number of shifts occur in verse 8. For the first time in the psalm David shifted from *talking to God* to *talking about God.* He shifted from focusing on the *works of God* to focusing on the *attributes of God.* That is, in verses 8-9 David shifted from the *greatness of God* to the *goodness of God.* The one who knows God is gracious and merciful understands God much better than the one who merely recognizes God is mighty. In his comments on verses 7-9, John Phillips (*Exploring the Psalms,* vol. 2, 652-653) pointed to the moral goodness of God (v. 7, "thy righteousness"), the merciful goodness of God (v. 8, "of great mercy"), and the manifold goodness of God (v. 9, "to all"). In verses 8-9 David also shifted from his own words to the words of Scripture. Verse 8 is almost a word-for-word repetition of God's self-revelation at Mount Sinai in Exodus 34:6-7. In fact, this is one of the most quoted sayings in the Old Testament (Num. 14:18; Neh. 9:17; Pss. 86:15; 103:8; 111:4; Joel 2:13; Jonah 4:2).

Five attributes of the Lord's nature are singled out. He is **gracious, full of compassion** ("compassionate," NIV; "merciful," NRSV, NASB), **slow to anger, of great mercy** ("rich in love," NIV), and **good to all.** The word **gracious** (*hannun*) stresses the undeserved nature of the favor God bestows. This adjective always refers to God in the Old Testament. It is used 13 times, and 11 of those times, as here, it is found in combination with **full of compassion.** The adjective translated **full of compassion** (*rahum*) also is used only of God in the Old Testament. **Slow to anger** literally reads "is long to anger." The *Revised English Bible* has "long-suffering." This shows God does not punish us immediately, as we deserve, but offers us time to repent. **Mercy** is the important word *hesed,* the Lord's "steadfast love" (NRSV), for which there is no exact English equivalent. And He is **great** or "rich" (NIV) in this merciful love. The *New American Standard Bible* reads "great in lovingkindness." Finally, the Lord is **good.**

The adjective **good** (*tob*) has moral overtones as well as implications of superior quality and worth. God's goodness is **to all.** This shows He is not interested merely in one group of people but cares for all people. This statement strikes the first of two quick notes of universalism—not a universalism of salvation but a universalism of God's goodness and His mercies. The next one follows immediately: **his tender mercies are over all his works. Tender mercies** ("compassion," NIV) is a form of the same word translated **compassion** in verse 8. As in verses 10 and 17, **all his works** refers to "all he has made" (see the NIV on vv. 9,10,17).

Does your mind wander during your time of daily personal worship? Focus on God and who He is. Let your mind be absorbed with Him. Let His greatness and goodness fill all your vision.

3. Tell Others About God (Ps. 145:10-12)

As a result of their worship, God's people are to go forth and tell others about God, His kingdom, and His mighty acts.

Verses 10-12: **All thy works shall praise thee, O Lord; and thy saints shall bless thee. They shall speak of the glory of thy kingdom, and talk of thy power; to make known to the sons of men his mighty acts, and the glorious majesty of his kingdom.**

The synonymous parallelism in these verses is obvious: **thy works ... thy saints; shall praise thee ... shall bless thee; speak of ... talk of; thy kingdom ... thy power; his mighty acts ... the glorious majesty of his kingdom.** In spite of this structure, however, there are subtle nuances in the text.

Verse 10 encompasses God's work both in creation and in redemption. **All thy works** is the same phrase as in verse 9: "all you have made" (NIV). **Thy saints** (*hasid*) are the redeemed ones who have entered into His covenant love (*hesed*). Together they constitute a chorus of praise.

But the emphasis of verses 10-13 is on God's rule rather than God's redemption. Four times the word **kingdom** (*malkut*) is used (vv. 11,12, and twice in v. 13). However, it is not merely God's

kingdom but **the glory of thy kingdom** and **the glorious majesty of his kingdom** that is emphasized. God's glory is centered in His glorious kingdom. And from these verses that speak of God's **saints** and His **power,** we understand that His kingdom is a kingdom of grace as well as a kingdom of might. It is this kingdom that inspires God's people to **talk** and to **speak; to make known** God and **his mighty acts** to others **(the sons of men).**

Hebrew manuscripts differ between the use of the second person (NIV) and the third person (KJV) in verse 12. That is, the manuscripts differ on whether David continued to talk *to God* or began to talk *about God.*

4. Expect God to Respond (Ps. 145:17-19)

David next affirmed that the Lord promises to respond to us by hearing our prayers and saving us when we call on Him truthfully and reverently.

Verses 17-19: **The Lord is righteous in all his ways, and holy in all his works. The Lord is nigh unto all them that call upon him, to all that call upon him in truth. He will fulfill the desire of them that fear him: he also will hear their cry, and will save them.**

In verse 17 God's two attributes, **righteous** and **holy,** balance each other. W. T. Purkiser said, "The righteousness and holiness of God are both the standard and the hope of man" ("The Book of Psalms," in the *Beacon Bible Commentary,* vol. 3 [Kansas City, Missouri: Beacon Hill Press, 1967], 441). And Willem VanGemeren noted: "His righteous acts are those of restoration, redemption, and vindication" ("Psalms," 863).

Righteous also could be translated "just" (NRSV). **Holy** is the word *hasid.* The *New International Version* translates it as "loving"; other versions have "kind" (NRSV, NASB, CEV). "Gracious" would be another good translation. The Hebrew word *hasid* is used 32 times in the Old Testament, 25 of which are in the Psalms. The word often is used of God's servants, His "saints" or "holy ones." In fact, the term became the designation of the Jewish orthodox party in the time of the Maccabeans. However, the word is used of God Himself only here in verse 17, in the additional part to verse 13b that appears in the *New International Version* but not in the *King James Version,* and in Jeremiah 3:12. **In all his works** could mean "toward all he has made" (NIV) or "in all His deeds" (NASB; similarly the REB, "in all he does").

Verse 18 shows us God is approachable. As soon as one begins to pray, the Lord is near or **nigh.** "Those who are members of His covenant fellowship are distinguished from the rest of His creation, because they 'call on him,' 'fear him,' and 'love him' (vv. 18-20)," wrote VanGemeren ("Psalms," 863). If the Lord is so good to His creation (v. 10) and to all people in general (v. 9), how much more will He care for those who are His people by redemption and covenant! Jesus made this same point in the Sermon on the Mount (Matt. 6:25-34). "The only qualification is an earnest need and an honest heart" (Purkiser, "The Book of Psalms," 441). **In truth** means "in sincerity" (REB) or "sincerely" (Moffatt). The *Contemporary English Version* reads, "You are near to everyone whose prayers are sincere."

The verbs in verse 19 can be translated as future tenses–**will fulfill, will hear, will save** (as in the KJV)–or as present tenses–**fulfills, hears, saves** (as in the NIV). **Save** means "delivers" (Tanakh).

Verse 19 is not a blanket promise. It is limited to **them that fear him. Fear him** means to "respect him" (NCV) or to "honor him" (TEV). For **them that fear him** the *Contemporary English Version* paraphrases, "all your worshipers." H. C. Leupold said, "True fear of God gives direction and limitation to prayers and prevents men from asking for things rashly, forgetting the nature of the Lord and His wholesome restraints" (*Exposition of the Psalms* [Grand Rapids: Baker Book House, 1969], 980).

When we as believers genuinely practice the spiritual discipline of personal worship, we can expect to experience God's presence and His effective action on our behalf.

June 22

GIVING

Basic Passages: Psalms 50:7-23; 66:8-15
Focal Passages: Psalms 50:7-13,23; 66:13-15

INTRODUCTION

1. As a Christian, giving is only putting your money into that to which you already have given yourself.

2. This lesson seeks to answer the question, "What kind of giving pleases God?"

3. The Central Bible Truth of this lesson is that believers are to be faithful and generous in their giving as an expression of their devotion to God.

4. The purpose of this lesson is to help you determine to cultivate the spiritual discipline of giving.

I. SOME PRELIMINARY CONSIDERATIONS

The Background

Psalm 50 is the first of twelve psalms titled "A Psalm of Asaph," "To Asaph," or "For Asaph." This is the only one of them in Book Two of the Psalter (Pss. 42–72); the other eleven (Pss. 73–83) are in Book Three (Pss. 73–89). If this is the same Asaph [AY-saf] as in the historical books, then he was selected to lead the music when David brought the ark into Jerusalem (1 Chron. 15:15-19). He was the chief musician under David (1 Chron. 16:4-5). He did significant work on beautifying the temple services (1 Chron. 25:1). And he also wrote sacred songs and psalms (2 Chron. 29:30). However, not all of the psalms in the Psalter that bear his name necessarily were written by Asaph. Some were written "for him" or "in honor of" his memory.

Psalm 66 is titled "To the chief Musician, A Song or Psalm." Only in this psalm and the next (Ps. 67) is this title used without indicating the author's name. No historical occasion or situation is indicated in the heading. Some have suggested that Psalm 66 commemorates the deliverance of Judah from the threat of the Assyrian conquest by Sennacherib [suh-NAK-uh-rib] in the time of King Hezekiah [HEZ-ih-kigh-uh] (2 Kings 18–19; Isa. 36–37). The psalm is a psalm of thanksgiving and moves from the corporate praise of the whole earth to that of Israel celebrating its redemption to that of one individual who brought his gift to the Lord and invited others to hear his story. As Derek Kidner (*Psalms 1–72,* in the Tyndale Old Testament Commentaries [London: Inter-Varsity Press, 1973], 233) said, the psalm "speaks of the God whose care is not only world- and nation-wide, but personal: 'I will tell what he has done for me' (v. 16)."

II. FOCAL PASSAGES EXAMINED
   (Pss. 50:7-13,23; 66:13-15)

That regular giving is a spiritual discipline is something many modern Christians have not yet grasped. This truth is something the psalmists had no trouble understanding.

1. Give Regularly (Ps. 50:7-8)

God expects all of His people to give to Him regularly out of their substance.
50:7: Hear, O my people, and I will speak; O Israel, and I will testify against thee: I am God, even thy God.
In this section of the psalm the Lord addressed the whole nation, **my people.** What made their sin so reprehensible was that they were God's own people. But God wanted not only to convict them; He wanted to heal them. They were **my people,** the covenant people, and He was **thy God.** These opening words seem to be designed deliberately to recall two Old Testament

events and passages: the opening of the Decalogue (Ex. 20:2; Deut. 5:6-7) and the Shema (Deut. 6:4-5).

The words **hear, I will speak,** and **I will testify against thee** indicate more than just that the Lord wanted the people to listen to Him. Rather, the scene is a courtroom. The prosecuting attorney and the judge are the Lord. The Lord has listened to them long enough. Now He will speak, and they are to listen. The word **hear** implies "obey."

50:8: **I will not reprove thee for thy sacrifices or thy burnt offerings, to have been continually before me.**

But before the Lord indicted the people on the charge of which they were guilty, He removed all misapprehension at the outset. He stated what they were *not* guilty of. God was not going to **reprove** or "rebuke" (NIV) the people for not bringing their **sacrifices** or **burnt offerings.** Why? Because they had been made **continually before me.** These people gave what was required of them, and they gave it regularly. They were regular in their giving! They were scrupulous in their giving. The law required **burnt offerings** to be made in both the morning and the evening. Thus every morning and every evening sacrifices could be seen burning on the altar. Further, burnt offerings belonged to the category of dedicatory offerings. In the burnt offering the whole of the animal was consumed on the altar, speaking of complete dedication to the Lord. These people gave the gift that was designed to show their total surrender to the Lord—but that was just what was lacking, their total surrender to the Lord.

Some of us don't even get as far as His ancient people did. We give only sporadically. At least they gave regularly. God did not condemn them for that. Indeed, He acknowledged they were right to give regularly to Him.

"Giving is a part of worship. When we go to church for corporate worship, we should likewise go for corporate giving. Thus we lay our total selves, person and property upon His altar. The obedient Christian will not attend church only once a month or twice a year. Neither should he give with the same spasmodic irregularity. A true worshiper will no more ignore the collection plate than he will refuse to sing during the song service, or to listen reverently to the reading of the Scriptures, or prayerfully to bow his head during prayer–all of which are parts of one whole–a genuine experience of worship. We jest, and often fret, over the man who sleeps during the sermon. But what about the man who looks the other way when the collection plate is passed? Both are failing to participate in the worship" (Herschel H. Hobbs, *The Gospel of Giving* [Nashville: Broadman Press, 1954], 40).

God's people are to cultivate the spiritual discipline of giving. However, merely giving to Him, even if that giving is on a regular basis, is not all God requires of His people.

2. Give Devotedly (Ps. 50:9-13,23)

God is not as concerned with the quantity we give to Him as He is with the quality of what we give to Him.

50:9-13: I will take no bullock out of thy house, nor he goats out of thy folds. For every beast of the forest is mine, and the cattle upon a thousand hills. I know all the fowls of the mountains: and the wild beasts of the field are mine. If I were hungry, I would not tell thee: for the world is mine, and the fullness thereof. Will I eat the flesh of bulls, or drink the blood of goats?

In these five verses God stated that He did not need, nor would He accept, their sacrifices. There is a note of sarcasm in the words **thy house** and **thy folds.** It is as if God heard them say, "My bull." "My goat." "My stall." "My pen." So He responded with, "No. Not yours. Mine!" God began His statement in verse 10 with an emphatic **mine** (*li*), and He ended it in verse 11 with **mine** (*'immadi*). As Creator of all, God owns all things. As Leupold (*Exposition of Psalms,* 393) said, "He is not a cattle buyer."

God identified four groups of animals as belonging to Him. The first two groups are **every beast of the forest** and **the cattle upon a thousand hills.** The familiar phrase **the cattle upon a**

thousand hills literally is "on the hills of the thousands." This phrase can be understood as referring to the cattle, not the hills–"upon the hills by the thousands." This is the way the *New English Bible* understands it, "and the cattle in thousands on my hills" (similarly the *Revised English Bible*). Or, it could refer to the hills, "the cattle on a thousand hills" (NIV). These words are the basis for the little chorus by John W. Peterson:

> He owns the cattle on a thousand hills
> The wealth in every mine
> He owns the rivers and the rock and rills,
> The sun and stars that shine.

One might own some of the beasts and cattle, but God owns more: **the fowls of the mountains** are His. No one can claim the birds of the air as his or her own–but God can. And more: **and the wild beasts of the field are mine.** This statement goes beyond what could have been sacrificed. It means "the creatures of the field" (NIV).

We cannot give God anything, for God owns everything. Verse 12 makes this clear: **for the world is mine, and the fullness thereof.** It is God who gives us what is His. All we have is a loan from Him. William W. How (1823-1897) recognized this when he wrote:

> We give Thee but Thine own,
> Whate'er the gift may be;
> All that we have is Thine alone,
> A trust, O Lord, from Thee.

("We Give Thee But Thine own," No. 609, *The Baptist Hymnal,* 1991.)

Some pagan peoples believed the gods were nourished and sustained by the sacrifices that were brought to them. But God does not need bulls and rams for this purpose. In verse 13 God asked, **Will I eat the flesh of bulls, or drink the blood of goats?** The obvious answer is "No!" God is not some hungry deity! But suppose for just a minute that God did need food to sustain Him. Even if He did need food to survive, God said, **If I were hungry, I would not tell thee.** God did not need them to feed Him or to keep Him content. "He did not reveal his laws on offerings and sacrifice in order to be 'fed'" (VanGemeren, "Psalms," 376). God wants relationships, not rituals. God did not need the sacrifices; the people needed them.

50:23: **Whoso offereth praise glorifieth me: and to him that ordereth his conversation aright will I show the salvation of God.**

The essence of the sacrificial system is found in giving praise to God. **Whoso offereth praise** means "He who sacrifices thank offerings." Giving **praise** or thanks is part of glorifying or honoring God. But true praise to God affects the life of the person who gives it. The phrase **ordereth his conversation aright** may mean "will order his conduct aright," referring to one's whole manner or way of life. To this person God will **show the salvation of God.** Or, the phrase could mean "he prepares the way so that I may show him the salvation of God" (NIV). That is, it may refer to walking in the path in which God would reveal His **salvation** (*yesaʿ*). God does not give salvation as a payback to those who give to Him.

But we moderns who chuckle at the idea that God needs to be fed should not slip into the error of thinking that God needs our praise or thanksgiving. God does not need our thanksgiving, as if He needed us to bolster His self-esteem. In the words of C. S. Lewis, God is not "like a vain woman wanting compliments" (*Reflections on the Psalms* [New York: Macmillan, 1958], 79). God wanted thanksgiving from His people because He wanted their lives to be full of joy. He wanted the richness of a relationship with His people. The significance of the offerings was in the heart attitude of the offerers. The offerings were to be expressions of gratitude and dedication to the Lord.

Those who give to God out of true devotion honor Him and open their lives to His saving work. The spiritual discipline of giving involves giving with a right heart. God's people are to honor Him by giving out of a spirit of true devotion. Such giving opens the way for understanding more about God.

3. Give Faithfully (Ps. 66:13-14)

Psalm 66 is a psalm of adoration. The psalm is divided into two major sections, clearly marked at verse 13 by the change in pronouns from the plural to the singular. Verses 13-20 focus on the psalmist's personal worship.

66:13-14: I will go into thy house with burnt offerings: I will pay thee my vows, which my lips have uttered, and my mouth hath spoken, when I was in trouble.

Too often we promise things to God; and then when the trouble has passed, we forget to do what we promised. Not so with this psalmist. In verse 13 we see the psalmist's resolve. He declared: **I will pay thee my vows.** Jonah used these same words, "I will pay that that I have vowed," when he made his vow to the Lord in the fish's belly in the depths of the sea (2:9).

Under Israel's laws a person was not required to make a vow. Vows often were made in times of adversity, when the believer asked the Lord to do something. In turn, the believer stated he would express his devotion to the Lord in an action that he would do as soon as God answered his prayers (see Judg. 11:30-40; Pss. 22:25; 61:8; 116:18; Jonah 2:9). Such was the case here. The psalmist made his vow **when I was in trouble.**

Vows, however, do not affect God's actions. God does not do something for us because we promise to do something for Him. He is not in the bargaining business. John Phillips (*Exploring the Psalms,* vol. 1, 531) wrote, "We can make all the pledges and promises we like to God but this will not alter His mind in any way. God is not to be bribed. Vows are voluntary. God does not ask for them, but once they are made they become binding. . . . To fail to keep our promises, whether to God or to man, always results in the deterioration of character."

The sacrifice was specified when one voluntarily made a vow to the Lord (Lev. 22:18-21). Usually, one offered thank offerings or communion offerings for a vow. In these offerings only the fat and parts of the animal were burned on the altar. The other parts of the thank offerings were given back to the worshiper and could be eaten by the worshiper and his friends in a *toda* or thanksgiving meal (see Lev. 3; 7:12-15; 22:29-30). The returned parts provided the basis for a feast and emphasized the joy of fellowship.

But the psalmist said he would offer **burnt offerings.** Burnt offerings were called *holocausts*–the whole of the animal was consumed on the altar and nothing was given back to the worshiper (Lev. 1). These offerings were Godward and spoke of total dedication to the Lord. They were not the kind that the worshiper and his friends shared in. This may be a hint that the psalm originally commemorated a very serious situation, or a great threat that had been removed, and the depth of the chastened worshiper's debt rather than the exuberant gratitude of a feast.

In response to God's goodness to them, believers need to be faithful in their giving to God. Just as the psalmist declared he would bring his offering **into thy house,** or temple, so should we. The local church is a good place to bring our offering to the Lord. "At the risk of being misunderstood, let me make a further statement. There are many Christian enterprises which constantly ask for our support. Some are good; others are questionable. Religious radio programs, traveling evangelists, and independent missionary enterprises comprise the bulk of these. Without the support of the members of our churches they could not exist. Yet, in many instances they are critical of our churches and the established programs which they foster. Hundreds of thousands of dollars are given annually to 'independents' over which the donors have absolutely no control. They publish no audits and make no reports. This is not to say that these groups are dishonest. What we are saying is that if giving to them is good, there is a better way. Our local churches are here to stay. We can call for an accounting of their stewardship, both in dollars and in doctrine. If the money given for these extraneous enterprises were brought into the storehouse, our local churches and established denominational institutions could do all and

more than is being accomplished by these who creep in un-
awares" (Hobbs, *The Gospel of Giving,* 44). Part of giving faithfully is to know where one's gift is going and how it will be used.

4. Give Generously (Ps. 66:15)

As David watched the people bringing their gifts for the build-
ing of the first temple, he praised the Lord in the presence of the
whole assembly, and said, "But who am I, and who are my people, that we should be able to give as generously as this? Everything comes from you, and we have given you only what comes
from your hand. . . . And now I have seen with joy how willingly
your people who are here have given to you. O Lord . . . keep
this desire in the hearts of your people forever, and keep their
hearts loyal to you" (1 Chron. 29:14,17-18). The depth of our devotion to the Lord is reflected in how generously we give to Him.
As Christians, we should give even more generously to Him because of His generosity to us.

66:15: **I will offer unto thee burnt sacrifices of fatlings,
with the incense of rams; I will offer bullocks with goats.
Selah.**

The word **Selah** occurs 71 times in the Psalter (and three
times in Habakkuk 3). Scholars are not certain what it indicated. Some have suggested it was a signal for an interlude or
change in the musical accompaniment. Others have suggested it
signaled an interjection or response such as "for ever" or "praise
the Lord." Attempts have been made to identify the root of the
word as "to lift up," indicating the lifting up of instruments or
voices, or as "to bend" or "to bow down," indicating the people
were to prostrate themselves at this point.

The psalmist said he would offer **fatlings, rams, bullocks,**
and **goats. Fatlings** are fat, healthy lambs. **Bullocks** are bulls.

The largess of the vow is unusual. The psalmist went beyond
what was required by the vow (see Lev. 1:3-13; 4:2-12; Num.
7:15,21,27; 15:2-16). The number and different types of animals

named may be another hint that this psalm originally commemorated a national rather than a personal deliverance. Further, **rams** were not offered as burnt offerings by the common people. They were offered by the high priest, by the king or prince acting as a representative of the people, or by a Nazarite. The fact that the psalmist made this kind of offering may be another indication he was the national leader. If this were King Hezekiah acting on behalf of the nation, that would explain the lavishness of the votive offering. On the other hand, the point may be that all the sacrifices one could make would not be enough to express proper praise to God, for these sacrifices speak of "total dedication and profound thankfulness" (Tate, "Psalms 51–100," 151).

Maybe you haven't been practicing the spiritual discipline of giving. Maybe you have not been giving regularly, devotedly, faithfully, or generously. You can change that today. An old proverb says, "A journey of a thousand miles begins with one step." Start by giving something. Take your first step this Sunday.

Because I have been given much, I, too, must give;
  Because of Thy great bounty, Lord, Each day I live,
I shall divide my gifts from Thee With ev'ry brother that I see
  Who has the need of help from me.

Because I have been sheltered, fed, By Thy good care,
  I cannot see another's lack And I not share
My glowing fire, my loaf of bread, My roof's safe shelter
    overhead,
  That he too may be comforted.

Because love has been lavished so Upon me, Lord,
  A wealth I know that was not meant For me to hoard,
I shall give love to those in need, Shall show that love by
    word and deed: Thus shall my thanks be thanks indeed.
(Grace Noll Crowell [1877-1969], "Because I Have Been Given Much," No. 605, *The Baptist Hymnal,* 1991).

June 29

WITNESSING

Basic Passage: Psalm 22:22-31
Focal Passage: Psalm 22:22-31

INTRODUCTION

1. In English, the word *witness* often is limited to one who observed an event. The biblical use of *witness* often involves attesting to something about which one is qualified to speak.
2. The Central Bible Truth of this lesson is that believers' witness concerning God's activity in their lives impacts people now and affects future generations.
3. The purpose of this lesson is to help you discover the importance of witnessing and commit to look for opportunities to tell others about Christ.
4. This lesson seeks to answer the question, Why is witnessing important?

I. SOME PRELIMINARY CONSIDERATIONS

1. The Titles

The Hebrew text of Psalm 22 begins with a title verse (which actually is v. 1 according to the Hebrew verse numbering). The title is printed above the psalm in the English versions and is not numbered. It has four parts that tell us four things.

The notation "To the chief Musician" (KJV) or "For the director of music" (NIV) is attached to fifty-five psalms and to the end of the psalm of Habakkuk (Hab. 3:19b). This heading suggests there was a collection of psalms, drawn together from different sources and choirs, that were compiled into a volume before the Psalter was completed.

"Upon *Aijeleth Shahar*" means "Set to 'The Hind of the Dawn.'" Some interpreters, including Martin Luther, think this is a glimpse of the psalm's theme, that help will come at daybreak. Probably, however, this is a musical direction that indicates the name of the melody or tune to which the song was to be sung. This is the way the *New International Version* understands the words by its rendering of the phrase "To the tune of 'The Doe of the Morning.'"

"A Psalm" (*mizmor*) probably indicates this poem was sung to instrumental accompaniment. It also may indicate it was a composition designed for a particular occasion. "Of David" indicates the authorship of the psalm, which we have no reason to doubt.

2. The Psalm's Messianic Nature

Psalm 22 is a messianic psalm. The New Testament directly quotes the psalm four times in relation to Jesus (v. 1 in Matt. 27:46 and Mark 15:34; v. 18 in John 19:24; and v. 22 in Heb. 2:12) and makes almost 20 other allusions or verbal parallels to it.

Psalm 22 has been called the fifth Gospel account of the crucifixion. Along with Isaiah 53, Psalm 22 shows the suffering Messiah more than any other Old Testament passage. The psalm begins with the words Jesus cried on the cross, "My God, my God, why hast thou forsaken me?" and it ends in the Hebrew language with a single word—"finished!" (*'asa*). When Jesus died, He uttered a single word in Greek—"Finished!" (*tetelestai,* John 19:30; "It is finished," KJV). "So the psalm begins with one word Jesus uttered on the cross and it ends with another (Phillips, *Exploring the Psalms,* vol. 1, 168).

II. FOCAL PASSAGE EXAMINED (Ps. 22:22-31)

Psalm 22 divides naturally into two parts. Verses 1-21 are an individual lament that centers around the theme of suffering. Verses 22-31 are a joyful song of thanksgiving over deliverance

received. The first half of Psalm 22 begins with a cry of despair
(v. 1); the second half begins with a shout of triumph (v. 22). Our
lesson focus only on the second half of the psalm.

1. Commitment to Witness (Ps. 22:22-23)

In verse 22 David told God what he would do. In verse 23
David told God's people what to do.

Verses 22-23: **I will declare thy name unto my brethren:
in the midst of the congregation will I praise thee. Ye that
fear the Lord, praise him; all ye the seed of Jacob, glorify
him; and fear him, all ye the seed of Israel.**

First, David told God what he would do. What David meant
by **I will declare thy name** is clarified by the parallel statement **will I praise thee.** This statement relates back to the
first half of the psalm. David's praise did not originate out of a
vacuum. His praise to God and what he would declare unto the
Lord's people involved telling them how the Lord answered his
cry for help. **My brethren** (*'ehay*) may refer to the psalmist's
relatives (as in Pss. 50:20; 69:8) or to his friends (as in Pss.
35:14; 122:8). But the Hebrew poetic parallelism indicates the
brethren are the same as **the congregation** (as in Ps. 133:1).
The congregation (*qahal*) is a technical term for the congregation of the righteous (see Pss. 107:32; 149:1), which excludes the
ungodly. In fact, the words **I will declare thy name unto my
brethren** are applied to Christ in Hebrews 2:11-12 in connection with His redeemed people.

In verse 23 David told God's people what to do. Three more titles are given for the congregation of the righteous. They are
identified as **ye that fear the Lord, ye the seed of Jacob,**
and **ye the seed of Israel.** Again, Hebrew poetic parallelism indicates these are not three separate groups but additional titles
for the congregation of verse 22.

The verbs **praise, glorify,** and **fear** indicate the outward expression of the fear of the Lord. In verse 23 two different He-

brew words are used for **fear.** In the title **ye that fear the Lord** the Hebrew word *yare'* may be translated as a noun, "you God-fearers." In the instruction to **fear him,** the Hebrew verb is *gur,* which means "to stand in awe of" or to "revere" (NIV). To **glorify** is to "honor" (NIV).

From these verses three important observations about witnessing can be drawn. First, witnessing begins with a commitment to witness. Believers need to determine what they will do. This is what David did. He said, **I will declare thy name.** Have you made a commitment to witness? That's where it all begins. Second, an important element in effective witnessing is sharing your testimony about God with fellow believers. Just as David's praise to God was not in isolation but through the believing community, so our witnessing must not be done in isolation from the church–for witnessing for God involves inviting people to become part of God's people, the body of Christ. Third, those who are committed to the spiritual discipline of witnessing encourage other believers to share their faith. All believers are to be witnesses for Christ. Sometimes it takes a little encouragement to get believers to do what they are supposed to be doing.

2. Reason to Witness (Ps. 22:24-26)

David's praise was both caused by and directed toward the Lord.
Verses 24-26: **For he hath not despised nor abhorred the affliction of the afflicted; neither hath he hid his face from him; but when he cried unto him, he heard. My praise shall be of thee in the great congregation: I will pay my vows before them that fear him. The meek shall eat and be satisfied: they shall praise the Lord that seek him: your heart shall live forever.**

The basis of David's reason to witness was what God had done for him. That is, David witnessed out of his own experience. David described God's help in three ways in verse 24. First, David said **he hath not despised nor abhorred the affliction**

of the afflicted. Second, he testified **neither hath he hid his face from him.** Third, David added **when he cried unto him, he heard.** All this, of course, goes back to the lament half of the psalm in verses 1-21. David praised God because he had experienced a total reversal of his predicament described in verses 1-2. David started with a feeling of forsakenness (v. 1), but now he knew God had **not despised** or **abhorred** his **affliction.** David began by crying out for help, but there seemed to be no answer to his cry (v. 2). Now he knew God **heard** and answered him.

Alternating his address to God and to the people, David again affirmed his intention of praising God **in the great congregation. My praise shall be of thee** literally reads "of thee my praise shall be." W. T. Purkiser said, "God is both the Object and the Source of His people's praise" ("The Book of Psalms," 192).

The words **I will pay my vows** refer to sacrificing a votive offering. A votive offering was a type of thank or peace offering that a worshiper vowed, or promised, to God in times of trouble (see Lev. 7:16-21; 22:21; Num. 15:8).

The meek literally are "the afflicted" (*'anaw*), a related word to **affliction** and **afflicted** in verse 24a. The *New International Version* reads "the poor." The Hebrew word "stresses the moral and spiritual condition of the godly as the goal of affliction implying that this state is joined with a suffering life rather than with one of worldly happiness and abundance." Thus this Hebrew word "expresses the intended outcome of affliction: humility" (Leonard J. Coppes, "*ana*," in the *Theological Wordbook of the Old Testament,* vol. 2, edited by R. Laird Harris, Gleason L. Archer, and Bruce K. Waltke [Chicago: Moody Press, 1980], 682). **The meek shall eat and be satisfied** refers to the participation of other afflicted ones with this formerly afflicted one in a communal meal that formed part of the ritual feast that symbolized fellowship with God.

Afflicted ones sharing with other afflicted ones is a characteristic of the poor or meek. This truth was driven home to me in the fall of 1983. I was a visiting scholar at Southern Baptist The-

ological Seminary in Louisville, Kentucky. Because my family
was not able to be with me and because I was on a limited bud-
get, I stayed in a dormitory room during the week. One of my
former students, an African-American, was enrolled at the seminary. One evening he and his wife wanted to take me out for dinner. I readily agreed, but said, "I should be taking you out to dinner, not your paying to take me out to dinner." I shall never
forget his response. He, referring to his wife and himself, said,
"Doc, we're too poor not to share what we have." Imagine that!
Too poor not to share! Most of us think that if we don't have
much we should hoard what we have and not share it with others. Our philosophy is "We have too little to share!" But here was
Christian meekness in action. And isn't that what witnessing is?
Someone has defined witnessing as "one beggar telling another
beggar where he can find bread." If you're one of the poor, the afflicted, the meek, you should have no trouble witnessing!

Satisfied (*sabea'*) is the usual verb for being filled with food.
This verb was used to describe the amount of manna the Israelites had each day—they were able to eat to the full (Ex. 16:8).
Yet here more than mere physical nourishment is meant. The afflicted would experience spiritual fullness in their lives as well.

The final phrase of verse 26, **your heart shall live forever,**
is a blessing: "May your hearts live forever!" (NIV). In the origi-
nal context of the fellowship meal, the phrase may be understood as a toast to the other diners.

Believers have many reasons for telling others what God has
done for them. They can and should tell how God has met their
needs when they called on Him for help. Primarily, believers are
to tell others how God has redeemed them through Christ.

3. Results of Witness (Ps. 22:27-29)

John Phillips (*Exploring the Psalms,* vol. 1, 173) pointed out
verses 27-29 concern the nations—their conversion (v. 27), control (v. 28), and content (v. 29).

Verses 27-29: **All the ends of the world shall remember
and turn unto the Lord: and all the kindreds of the nations shall worship before thee. For the kingdom is the
Lord's: and he is the governor among the nations. All
they that be fat upon earth shall eat and worship: all they
that go down to the dust shall bow before him: and none
can keep alive his own soul.**

All the ends of the world is a parallel expression to **all the
kindreds of the nations.** The former refers to the remotest
corners of the globe. The latter literally is "all the families of the
nations" (NIV). This recalls the Abrahamic covenant that was
for "all families of the earth" (Gen. 12:3; see Ps. 96:7).

Shall remember does not refer to recalling something that
previously was known and not retained in mind. Rather, this re-
membrance involves an act of obeisance and worship. They shall
turn unto the Lord and **shall worship before thee.**

In verse 28 the nations recognize the true Ruler and His dominion: **the kingdom is the Lord's,** or "dominion belongs to
the Lord" (NIV), and **he is the governor among the nations,**
or "he rules over the nations" (NIV).

Verse 29 is difficult to understand. Among those David saw as
comprising the worshiping community would be **they that be
fat upon earth** and **they that go down to the dust.** Perhaps
David was referring to the living and the dead respectively in
the two halves of this verse. Or perhaps he was referring to
those who at present are self-sufficient and to those who are not.
In that case, the first group, **they that be fat upon earth,** are
"the rich of the earth" (NIV; Hebrew, *disne*), or prosperous people and nations. The second group, **they that go down to the
dust,** involve "those who are fainthearted, sickly, dying, and
filled with anguish, even as the psalmist once lay 'in the dust of
death' (v. 15; cf. 30:3)" (VanGemeren, "Psalms," 211). These are
described further as those among whom **none can keep alive
his own soul.** The point then is "both well-fed and poor people
will join in the worship of God" (VanGemeren, "Psalms," 211).

Witnessing to what God has done for you in front of fellow believers is important. Witnessing, however, cannot stop there. When God's people move outside the congregation to share what God has done for them in Christ, people in all parts of the world will come to Him. Isaac Watts wrote of this in his hymn "Jesus Shall Reign Where'er the Sun" (No. 282, *Baptist Hymnal,* 1975).

> Jesus shall reign where'er the sun
> Does his successive journeys run,
> His kingdom spread from shore to shore
> Till moons shall wax and wane no more.

> From north to south the princes meet
> To pay their homage at His feet,
> While western empires own their Lord
> And savage tribes attend His word.

4. Continuation of Witness (Ps. 22:30-31)

Verses 30-31 move from the universal extent of witnessing to the future extent of witnessing.

Verses 30-31: **A seed shall serve him; it shall be accounted to the Lord for a generation. They shall come, and shall declare his righteousness unto a people that shall be born, that he hath done this.**

The picture of one generation, as it were, passing the baton to the next is found in both the Old Testament and the New Testament (Deut. 6:20-25; 2 Tim. 2:2). Here **a seed** refers to "posterity" (NIV). **A generation** actually is "future generations" (NIV). **A people that shall be born** is "a people yet unborn" (NIV).

What is to be declared to those coming after us? What is the content of our witness for the Lord? The psalmist helped us: we are to **declare his righteousness,** and we are to testify **he hath done this.** The word for **righteousness** (*sedaqa*) means "justice" or "deliverance." The word is used in the Old Testament of God's saving action, of rescuing His covenant people, of delivering His people. It refers to God's saving and vindicating His people because He is faithful and keeps His covenant promises. Rescue, salvation, and victory all are involved in the meaning of this term. The English translation does not do justice to the Hebrew for **he hath done this**. **He hath done this** is only one word in the Hebrew (*'asa*). This word is used in the Old Testament of God's mighty acts, His intervention in history. The word often is used of the signs and wonders He performed in the course of history (Josh. 24:17; Ps. 98:1; Isa. 25:1). What is it then that **he hath done**? The Lord has brought salvation to us!

We have heard the joyful sound: Jesus saves! Jesus saves!
  Spread the tidings all around: Jesus saves! Jesus saves!
Bear the news to ev'ry land, Climb the steeps and cross
    the waves;
  Onward! 'tis our Lord's command; Jesus saves! Jesus saves!

Waft it on the rolling tide: Jesus saves! Jesus saves!
  Tell to sinners far and wide: Jesus saves! Jesus saves!
Sing, ye islands of the sea; Echo back, ye ocean caves;
  Earth shall keep her jubilee: Jesus saves! Jesus saves!

Give the winds a mighty voice: Jesus saves! Jesus saves!
  Let the nations now rejoice: Jesus saves! Jesus saves!
Shout salvation full and free; Highest hills and deepest caves;
  This our song of victory: Jesus saves! Jesus saves!
(Priscilla Owens, "We Have Heard the Joyful Sound," No. 581, *The Baptist Hymnal*, 1991.)

What is the impact of our witness on posterity? It is seen by the future generations' response—they **shall serve him.** Sooner or later we all will die. But believers who cultivate the spiritual discipline of witnessing have the opportunity to impact not only their own generation; they have the opportunity to impact generations to come. We will die, but what God has done will continue to be told from generation to generation until the Lord returns (Matt. 16:18). Witness to someone today!

UNIT II: Psalms for Times of Crisis

July 6

WHEN IN NEED OF COMFORT

Basic Passage: Psalm 23
Focal Passage: Psalm 23:1-6

INTRODUCTION

1. When people are in need or facing crisis situations, they often turn to the Psalms for comfort. Indeed, many of the psalms are helpful to people in crisis situations.

2. Today we begin a new unit of study, "Psalms for Times of Crisis." The lessons studied in this four-session unit are designed to help those in need of comfort, encouragement, forgiveness, and protection.

3. The Central Bible Truth of this lesson is that God is ever present to comfort and to provide for His people in crises.

4. The purpose of this lesson is to help you understand and determine to rely on God's promise of comfort in crises.

5. This lesson seeks to answer the question, Where is God when I hurt?

I.   SOME PRELIMINARY CONSIDERATIONS

1. The Background

The superscription of Psalm 23 attributes it to David. Tradition does the same. There is no reason to question this understanding. In beautiful, simple poetry, Psalm 23 is the autobiography of one who trusted God in every experience of life and found Him trustworthy. Psalm 23 has a universal quality that lets it speak to the ages, for it speaks the language of the heart.

2. The Psalm of Comfort

Kyle M. Yates (*Preaching from the Psalms* [Nashville: Broadman Press, 1948], 64) wrote, "This is indeed the pearl of the Psalms, a nightingale singing in the world's night of loneliness and need." It is no wonder that its six brief verses are the most widely known and loved of all the psalms.

Throughout life, crises arise. Some are more severe than others. Some crises–such as a serious illness, the death of a loved one, or a divorce–can be so devastating that they overwhelm the person involved. At times like these, people need a place to turn to find words of comfort.

Strangely enough, even those without a religious commitment often turn to the Psalms for comfort–particularly to Psalm 23. Throughout my pastoral experience, Psalm 23 has been requested for use at funerals more than any other Scripture. And yet this psalm speaks to us all through life as well as in the hour of crisis or death. Indeed, if this psalm has no meaning to us in life, it will have no real meaning for us in death. For it is not the beauty of the words that brings us true comfort; it is the beautiful Lord of whom the words speak who comforts us.

II. FOCAL PASSAGE EXAMINED (Ps. 23:1-6)

Derek Kidner wrote of this short "Shepherd Psalm": "Depth and strength underlie the simplicity of this psalm. Its peace is not escape; its contentment is not complacency: there is a readiness to face deep darkness and imminent attack, and the climax reveals a love which homes towards no material goal but to the Lord Himself" (*Psalms 1-72,* 109).

1. The Provision (Ps. 23:1-3)

In verses 1-4 David used a sheep-shepherd analogy to describe the trusting relationship between the believer and God.

Verse 1: **The Lord is my shepherd; I shall not want.**

Verse 1 is the key verse of the entire psalm. The words **the Lord** translate *Yahweh,* the divine name that in English is rendered "Jehovah" or LORD (in small capital letters). It is the name used to designate the true God. It is God's saving name. By it He revealed Himself to Moses as the one who would redeem Israel from Egyptian bondage (Ex. 3:7-15). The word *Yahweh* or LORD is formed from the Hebrew verb "to be." "I AM THAT I AM" in Exodus 3:14 reads, literally, "He will be that [which] He will be." God revealed Himself in His deepest nature as Redeemer. Thus the idea may be summed up in the reading, "The redeeming God is my Shepherd; I shall not want."

"The *Lord* is my shepherd." "The Lord is my *shepherd.*" "The Lord *is* my shepherd." "The Lord is *my* shepherd." Each of these emphases adds meaning to this sublime truth. However, the emphasis placed on "my" and then "I" makes the statement not merely a principle but a personal avowal of faith. The fact that "the Lord is *my* shepherd" gives a logical basis for the faith expressed in **I shall not want.** Since the Lord was David's shepherd, he was not in want for any of his needs. *Needs,* not *luxuries,* are the content of this faith. The Lord supplies the necessities of life for those who trust in Him. Most of all, He supplies His comfort and grace.

Verse 2: **He maketh me to lie down in green pastures: he leadeth me beside the still waters.**

Early each morning the shepherd led his sheep from the fold. Dewdrops like millions of diamonds sparkled from every blade of grass. The early morning sun turned the landscape into a treasurehouse of beauty. But this beauty served also the practical purpose of making the grass juicy, succulent, and tender. The figure of **green pastures** was most meaningful in a land where such luxuriant graze was scarce. The shepherd found the best pastures and led his sheep to them. There the sheep would eat to the full, lie down, and then rise to eat again. No hunting or scrounging for a few blades of grass here and there. The green pasture was in abundance, far beyond the needs of the grazing sheep.

After the sheep had eaten their fill and the sun's heat bore down on them, the shepherd would lead them to **still waters.** There they could quench their thirst by the quiet water.

The primary thought in verse 2 is *filling* and *refreshment.* Just as the shepherd does for his sheep, God provides for all the needs of those who are His.

Verse 3: He restoreth my soul: he leadeth me in the paths of righteousness for his name's sake.

Having drunk their fill, the sheep were allowed to rest and relax in that quiet place. As they rested, the shepherd watched over them. He also moved among them looking for diseased or torn places on their bodies. These sores or wounds he treated so the sheep might heal. In other words, he restored them.

In like fashion, Jesus is called the Good Shepherd in the New Testament (John 10:11-18). The Good Shepherd leads His sheep into quiet repose. He refreshes their lives and restores their souls, removing by forgiveness their blemishes and tenderly healing their hurts. What a blessed thing it is—filled and refreshed—to lie down to rest under the watchful protection of our Good Shepherd, to be cleansed and restored spiritually.

In this hustle-and-bustle age, Christians need to be alone with their Shepherd. We need to escape the strain and tension of a demanding world. We need to be like the mother of a large family who labored long and hard throughout the day taking care of her children but late in the afternoon would slip away from the noise of the home to give her weary body and frayed nerves a quiet time under an old oak tree. Then, refreshed by meditation and prayer, she returned to her task. Out of this daily experience came her words:

I love to steal a while away,
From every encumbering care,
And spend the hours of departing day
In humble, reverent prayer.

She knew from practice what every Christian should know: **He restoreth my soul.**

The Hebrew words for **restoreth my soul** literally mean, "He brings back my life." The expression was used to illustrate spiritual restoration, often in terms of a stray sheep being brought back (as in Isa. 49:5). Jesus used a beautiful example of this action in Matthew 18:12-13. But **restoreth** also had a physical and psychological sense to it (as in Isa. 58:12, Prov. 25:13, and Lam. 1:11,16,19). Are you exhausted from what life has done to you? The Good Shepherd can make you feel that life is good and worth living. He can give you back the enjoyment of life. In all senses, the Good Shepherd retrieves, revives, renews, and refreshes His sheep.

Furthermore, the Shepherd leads **in the paths of right-eousness for his name's sake.** That is, He leads in paths that are in keeping with His name "Jehovah." What are these paths? They are the right paths. For literal sheep, the right paths were the safe paths. For the Good Shepherd's human flock, the words demand a moral content. **The paths of righteousness** are not paths that lead to the obtaining of **righteousness** (*sedeq*). Rather, these are the straight paths as opposed to the crooked paths (Ps. 125:5; Prov. 2:15; 5:6; 10:9).

In these verses David focused on the provision the Shepherd provided him as his Care-giver, Provider, Protector, and Guide. This was how David experienced the grace and goodness of his Shepherd. Is this your experience in your relationship with the Good Shepherd?

2. The Presence (Ps. 23:4)

David not only knew the provision of his Shepherd, he knew the presence of his Shepherd as well.

Verse 4: **Yea, though I walk through the valley of the shadow of death, I will fear no evil: for thou art with me; thy rod and thy staff they comfort me.**

One day while we were driving from Jericho to Jerusalem through the wilderness of Judea, the guide pointed toward a foreboding canyon. "There," said he, "is the valley of the shadow of death." Certainly David had some similar valley in mind. At times it was necessary for the shepherd to lead his sheep through such a canyon to take them to the green pasture beyond. In such a place shadows abounded, the terrain was rough and dangerous, and lurking within the shadows or beyond every turn might be some wild beast or evil men. But the sheep followed, unafraid as the shepherd led, his shepherd's **rod** and **staff** ever at the alert to ward off danger. If wild animals or evil men threatened, his **rod** was ready to drive them off. With his **staff** the shepherd guided timorous and erring sheep. Should one fall into a hole, the shepherd used the staff to pull the sheep to safety. The rod and staff were a continuous **comfort** to the sheep.

This verse usually is associated with the idea of death–but it speaks primarily to life. The Hebrew word rendered **shadow of death** means, literally, "deep shadow." Throughout life one can expect to walk through valleys of deep, dark shadows: anguish, bereavement, disease, distress, heartache, pain, and sorrow. In such times the Christian should walk with soul serenity, for the believer does not walk alone. Did you notice there was a change of person in verse 4? Prior to this David was talking *about God.* When he came to walking through **the valley of the shadow of death,** David began to talk *to God*–**thou art with me.**

One cannot, however, view life's crises without taking into account the hour of death. If the Lord delays His return, everyone engaged in this Bible study will tread that path. But you need not walk into that valley alone. The Savior has been this way before. In death as in life, He is the Good Shepherd. Not one of His sheep will be lost from Him. When His children enter that valley–afraid, perhaps, for they have not passed that way before–they find One who stays with them. Notice the text does not say the Shepherd leads His sheep *to* the valley. Nor does it say He only leads them *into* the valley. It says He leads

them *through* the valley. On the other side of the dark valley
are rich pastures and quiet streams to which those of earth
cannot compare. Sorrow and death are dark valleys, but neither sorrow nor death are blind *alleys*; they are *thoroughfares*
into blessings untold. God may not always keep you from the
dark valleys, but He will go with you through those valleys. His
presence will be with you to comfort you.

Are you in need of comfort today? Reread verses 1-4 and repeat after me: "I shall not want for complete satisfaction. I shall
not want for guidance. I shall not want for renewal. I shall not
want for instruction in righteousness. I shall not want for
courage in danger. I shall not want for God's presence with me. I
shall not want for comfort in sorrow" (modified from W. T.
Purkiser's outline of verses 1-4, "Psalms," *Beacon Bible Commentary,* vol. 3, 194-195). Now, what is it you were in want for?

3. The Preparation (Ps. 23:5)

In verses 5-6 David changed the metaphor from that of the
tender shepherd with his sheep to that of the gracious host and
his guests. This was another familiar figure drawn from ancient
life, except that it is one of even greater intimacy. Here we have
moved from the field to the home. The Lord is shown to be the
unparalleled Host.

Verse 5: **Thou preparest a table before me in the presence of mine enemies: thou anointest my head with oil;
my cup runneth over.**

Some interpreters understand the words **in the presence of
mine enemies** to refer to defeated enemies and see this as a
victory celebration where the enemies are present as captives.
On the other hand, the New Testament often pictures heaven,
according to Jewish thought, as a great banquet. However, no
enemies will be there. In the Ancient Near East, when a guest
entered a host's home, the guest enjoyed not only the host's hospitality but also his protection. This means the setting David

had in mind was on earth, not in heaven. The Lord is pictured
as spreading a sumptuous feast, **a table,** before His people even
while they are surrounded by their enemies. David saw life as a
great feast, even though he was beset by his foes. Under the protection of his great Host, David knew he was safe from evil.
Even if his way at times seemed hard, the Lord sustained and
nourished David so that no harm befell him outside the Lord's
will. David was able to enjoy the meal in peace because of the
presence of his Host. This is the promise to everyone who trusts
in the Lord.

Furthermore, the Host singled out David for special recogni-
tion and honor: **thou anointest my head with oil.** This does
not mean that only David received this honor. He was speaking
of his own experience, but such is true of all the Lord's guests.
In other words, God knows and cares for each one of His own.
Thus, with David each one should be elated with boundless joy.
Each one should be able to testify, **My cup runneth over.**
David's joy knew no bounds. He could not contain it. Our cups
should not only be full; they should overflow. God is an extrava-
gant Host.

What are opposition and difficulties to believers when their
Host is taking care of them? Here is "cool assurance under pressure." As Derek Kidner wrote, "It is one thing to survive a
threat, as in verse 4; quite another to turn it into triumph"
(*Psalms 1-72,* 111-112).

4. The Pursuit (Ps. 23:6)

God aggressively pursues His people with His goodness and
steadfast love.

Verse 6: **Surely goodness and mercy shall follow me all
the days of my life: and I will dwell in the house of the
Lord forever.**

Because of what the Lord had done in the past, David looked
with confidence to the future. The good God had provided, and

His unchanging love, David said, **shall follow me all the days of my life.** David was referring to his life on earth. Whatever experiences might come, whether good or bad, he could look back and see God's **goodness** (*tob*) and **mercy** (*hesed;* covenant love, "love," NIV) in it. Here **follow** does not mean "following after," as if goodness and mercy were bringing up the rear; it means "to pursue." Even as God's judgments pursue the wicked (Ps. 83:15), so His goodness and lovingkindness pursue the righteous.

This psalm raises an important issue. If God's goodness and love follow believers all the days of their lives, why shouldn't His comfort be self-evident? Why should a believer need to ask, "Where is God when I hurt?"

Crises often are prolonged events in a person's life. And God's comfort often is not self-evident. Too often believers tend to equate comfort with pain relief and deliverance, or we expect a quick fix, a name-it-and-claim-it response, or a formulaic answer. But God's comfort does not always relieve the pain or deliver His people from their crises. When understood in the context of God's character and will, however, God's comfort does bring hope, encouragement, strength, and peace. Saints through the ages testify to this fact. Though the loving Heavenly Father may permit His children to walk over rough paths, His presence is there. One may not always understand the event of the moment, but looking back the believer can see God's protecting and shaping hand in it. He works for good for all who love Him and who follow His will (Rom. 8:28).

Mercifully, the Lord does not unveil future events in one's life. If He did, even stalwart hearts would faint. But one by one, step by step, He leads His children along. Surmounting one difficulty leads to trust in God for the next. Such trust is evidence of a developing spiritual maturity.

But the prospect also reaches out into endless eternity. Some interpreters limit the meaning of **I will dwell in the house of the Lord forever** to David's desire for a permanent residence in the temple in Jerusalem or to a promise that he would return to the house of the Lord, rendering the Hebrew: "I shall come back to the house of the Lord as long as I live." While the Hebrew for **forever** literally is "to length of days," limiting David's meaning to his own lifetime is to ignore this is an obvious reference to heaven. It is also to ignore the fact that the temple was not built in David's day.

Compounded beyond measure will be the comfort and support the Lord's people know on earth. Human language cannot describe it. But when all the superlatives are exhausted, there is more comfort for the beyond–**I will dwell in the house of the Lord forever.**

WHEN IN NEED OF ENCOURAGEMENT

Basic Passage: Psalms 42:1–43:5
Focal Passages: Psalms 42:1-4,6-7; 43:3-5

INTRODUCTION

1. At times each of us feels the sentiment expressed in these psalms. Intellectually we know God is present everywhere, but spiritually He seems to be far away. Such a feeling produces a sense of loneliness of soul that defies expression in mere words. Perhaps it may happen in some crisis of sorrow when grief seems to be overwhelming. Or perhaps it may be in a time of temptation or trial, a time when you sense an unusual need for God, that you will long for some tangible evidence of His presence—but find none. In such times, faith is confronted by doubt. Our souls become battlegrounds between the two. Hope is beset by discouragement, and we find ourselves in a tug-of-war between them. We are caught, as it were, in the roaring waters of a turbulent stream in which we fight the elements in a life-and-death struggle. At the very moment when we feel our feet upon a rock on which we can stand with our heads above the water, we are swept from it and must continue the struggle. To such people on such occasions these psalms speak with a word of encouragement.

2. The Central Bible Truth of this lesson is that God encourages His people when they turn to Him in crises that threaten to overwhelm them.

3. The purpose of this lesson is to help you identify ways God can encourage you in crises.

4. This lesson seeks to answer the question, How can I overcome my discouragement?

I. SOME PRELIMINARY CONSIDERATIONS

1. The Background

Among commentators there is virtual agreement that Psalms 42–43 originally were one psalm. Several Hebrew manuscripts combine them into one psalm. Psalm 43 does not have a title; Psalm 42 does. The theme, style, and language of the two psalms are similar. The recurring refrain in 42:5, 42:11, and 43:5 marks the ends of the three stanzas.

As with 55 of the psalms, Psalm 42 is labeled "To the chief Musician" (KJV) or "For the director of music" (NIV) in the superscription. This heading suggests there was a collection of psalms that had been drawn together from different sources that were compiled into a volume before the biblical Psalter was completed.

Psalm 42 also is labeled a *Maschil* [MAHS-keel] (KJV) or *Maskil* (NIV). The term, used in connection with 13 psalms, is the participle of a verb that means "to make wise" or "to be prudent." The translators of the Greek translation of the Old Testament, the Septuagint, understood these as psalms of insight, instruction, and understanding. However, most of the psalms so labeled are not wisdom psalms. Thus the term's use in the headings is uncertain.

The "sons of Korah" were the descendants of Korah. Korah was a grandson of Levi (Ex. 6:16,18,21,24). Heman, one of the three principal singer-conductors of David's time (1 Chron. 15:17; 2 Chron. 5:12), was a descendant of Korah (1 Chron. 6:33). John I Durham ("Psalms," *The Broadman Bible Commentary,* vol. 4 [Nashville: Broadman Press, 1971], 256) suggested that the sons of Korah were the singers, conductors, and composers associated with David's approach to psalmody in Jerusalem. Twelve psalms in the Psalter are ascribed to this levitical family.

2. Memory, the Storehouse of Experience

As you study Psalms 42–43, notice the vital role the psalmist's memory played in strengthening him during a time of distress. When God seemed far away, the psalmist recalled the times when He seemed so near.

This suggests the importance of storing up in the mind experiences that give help in the day of struggle. If you would have pleasant memories tomorrow, you must have wholesome experiences today. To trust God in the sunshine enables us to find in Him refuge in the storm. You cannot feed the body from an empty cupboard; neither can you feed the soul today from a wasted past. It behooves all of us, therefore, to store up in our memories our experiences with God in times of joy in order that His presence may be real to us in times of discouragement and depression. Remember, one who does not learn to sing in the day scarcely will find a song to sing in the night.

II. FOCAL PASSAGES EXAMINED
(Pss. 42:1-4,6-7; 43:3-5)

When the bottom falls out of our lives or life falls in on us, we tend to ask, Why? Such should not cause Christians shame when we recall that on the cross even Jesus asked, "My God . . . why?" (Matt. 27:46; Mark 15:34). Those who have a disposition to believe have no need to fear doubt, for those with such a disposition will struggle through their doubts to an affirmation of faith.

1. Desire (Ps. 42:1-2)

In poetic language the psalmist painted a picture of spiritual drought. He portrayed a grim scene of spiritual hunger, loneliness, persecution, and overwhelming trouble. Yet throughout his plaintive utterance is the affirmation that God is the source of encouragement to His people.

42:1-2: **As the hart panteth after the water brooks, so panteth my soul after thee, O God. My soul thirsteth for God, for the living God: when shall I come and appear before God?**

Thirst is the most driving of all our appetites. One can live for weeks without food; but in a desert locale, one can live only a matter of days–if that–without water. Palestine is an arid land, with rainfall limited to spring and late fall. During the rainy seasons water holes can be found and brooks are available. But with the coming of the dry seasons these soon dry up.

Picture a **hart** or "deer" (NIV) wandering here and there in search of water. The deer goes to places where water once was found, but no longer. The dry holes and wadi beds only mock its search. Finally it comes to a place where at a former time it had drunk from a refreshing brook. The dry sand only makes its thirst all the greater. It paws in the sand, but not even a damp spot is found. The poor deer only can stand and pant in a frenzy in the barren waste. Every cell in its body longs for moisture. Almost to the point of panic, it turns its head hither and yon, longing for thirst-quenching water–but none is found.

As the deer thirsts for water, so did the psalmist thirst for God. Twice he stated it: **so panteth my soul after thee, O God** and **My soul thirsteth for God.** Literally, **panteth** reads "longs for." In times past the psalmist's experiences with God had been as that of the deer during the rainy seasons, but now his experience was akin to the deer's search for water in a dreary land. As the deer, the psalmist saw himself coming to a dry hole. The psalmist's thirst, however, was a thirst of **soul** after **God: My soul thirsteth for God, for the living God.** A person who lives only for the flesh scarcely can know this longing, but one with finely tuned spiritual senses knows it. For emphasis the psalmist added **the living God.** This is the first time this term appears in the Psalms. It contrasts the true God to the false gods around him, the living God with dead idols.

In the figure of the deer we see the anxious thirst of the psalmist for fellowship with God. The psalmist asked, **When**

shall I come and appear before God? In its historical context, this was a reference to worshiping in the temple. The *New International Version* reads, "When can I go and meet with God?" The psalmist knew he was experiencing the drought. Nevertheless, his desire was toward God. And so it should be for us. As God's people we need to recognize God as the source of encouragement and seek His help in trying times. Are you discouraged? Are you in need of encouragement? If so, then is your desire for God?

2. Distress (Ps. 42:3-4)

Have you ever been so discouraged and distressed that you cried all the time and didn't want to eat? Our psalmist was.

42:3: **My tears have been my meat day and night, while they continually say unto me, Where is thy God?**

So terrible was the psalmist's condition that he lost his appetite. His only **meat,** or "food" (NIV), was tears that ran down his cheeks into his mouth **day and night. Day and night** expresses a constant state. He had no relief from his sad condition.

Added to this was his enemies' taunting question: **Where is thy God?** Such repeated taunting probably planted doubts and questions in his own heart. Where was God when these things happened to him? Did God know about him? Did He care? If He knew and cared, was He powerless to act on his behalf?

The same hobgoblins of doubt beset all of us when life goes awry. We are plagued with doubts and questions the devil plants in our minds. At one time or another every child of God knows what has been called "the dark night of the soul." And in such a night, doubts—like bats—fill the air.

But the psalmist's state of desolation provided opportunity for him to demonstrate his faith in God. And his testimony was all the more effective because of the conditions surrounding it.

We too are stewards of our sorrow and suffering. If taken in the proper spirit, they become pulpits from which to declare our faith in God and to show forth His glory.

42:4: **When I remember these things, I pour out my soul in me: for I had gone with the multitude, I went with them to the house of God, with the voice of joy and praise, with a multitude that kept holyday.**

When the psalmist could find neither hope in the present nor a logical answer to give to his tormentors, he resorted to memory. He poured out the memories of the past within himself. By his memory he was lifted out of his present predicament and transmitted through time and space to happier circumstances. Out of his treasurehouse of memory the psalmist drew courage and strength. He remembered an occasion when the people **kept holyday,** or one of the religious feasts of Israel. Before his mind there loomed a happy, rejoicing, worshiping throng approaching the temple in Jerusalem. He was a part of it–indeed, the *New International Version* says he was "leading the procession." The songs and prayers echoed in his soul. God's presence was so real then. This joyful occasion overshadowed his present predicament. And this recollection kindled new hope that eventually he would know God's nearness once again.

Jean Paul Richter said, "Recollection is the only paradise from which we cannot be turned out" (Ely, *I Quote,* 224). Through remembering meaningful and joyful worship experiences with God's people, believers can be encouraged that God has worked in their lives in the past and that He can do so again.

3. Discouragement (Ps. 42:6-7)

High spiritual aspirations and resolutions often are followed by periods of discouragement. Just as one seems to be rising above trouble, Satan assails again.

42:6-7: **O my God, my soul is cast down within me: therefore will I remember thee from the land of Jordan, and of the Hermonites, from the hill Mizar. Deep calleth unto deep at the noise of thy waterspouts: all thy waves and thy billows are gone over me.**

Here the psalmist changed his figure from a waterless waste to water so plentiful that it inundated him. Evidently he was in the foothills of Mount Hermon. Mount Hermon is the source of the Jordan River–this **land of Jordan. Hermonites** is literally "the Hermons," the foothills of the mountain. The *New International Version* reads "the heights of Hermon." **The hill Mizar** [MIGH-zahr] has not been identified. The name means "the mountain of littleness" and probably was one of the lesser peaks in the Hermon range. The area described is the place to which David fled from Absalom (2 Sam. 17:22).

The psalmist still was held in the viselike grip of discouragement. **The noise of thy waterspouts** should read "the roar of your waterfalls" (NIV). Mount Hermon is 9,200 feet high, the tallest mountain in Palestine. Even in portions of the summertime its peak is covered with snow. The waterfalls were produced by the melting snow, the water of which rushed down the mountain. In the foothills of Mount Hermon the psalmist constantly heard the roar of the waterfalls crashing down from the higher peaks and echoing and reechoing through the canyons and gorges of the foothills. The thunderous sound of the waterfalls and the deluge of water only served to remind him of the raging sea. In his depression and despair he felt he was being sucked beneath the sea's stormy waves and swallowed up. All God's **waves** and **billows** had swept over him. The author piled figure upon figure to describe the new onrush of discouragement and depression that engulfed him. He was overwhelmed with discouragement. He was drowning under it. But out of the depths he cried to God, even though at the moment God seemed to be far away. Tossed in the storm, as it were, his faith still held on to God. And God had not deserted him.

4. Deliverance (Ps. 43:3-5)

The psalmist was still in a state of trouble. He had his ups and downs. Outwardly his circumstances had not changed, but

in faith he rested his case in God's hands. He put his hope in
God. His faith won through.

**43:3: O send out thy light and thy truth: let them lead me;
let them bring me unto thy holy hill, and to thy tabernacles.**

In this spirit the psalmist implored God for His **light** and
truth. Light is synonymous with God's presence (Num. 6:25; Ps.
80:1,3,7,19). God's truth is the opposite of all lies or falseness, as
His light is the opposite of all darkness. So the psalmist prayed
that God's presence would drive away the darkness of despair,
and that His truth would confound the false accusations of his
foes. He longed to go to God's **holy hill**—Jerusalem—and to His
tabernacles, or abiding place—the temple where God was said
to dwell in mercy with His people. God's light and truth would
lead him there.

**43:4: Then will I go unto the altar of God, unto God my
exceeding joy: yea, upon the harp will I praise thee, O
God my God.**

The psalmist promised that on arrival he would go to God's
altar in the temple. He exclaimed God was his **exceeding joy,**
or "my joy and my delight" (NIV). Going to God's altar meant he
would get as close to God's presence as possible. No one appreci-
ates the sense of God's presence as much as one who has felt
bereft of it. Furthermore, in contrast to the dirges he had been
chanting, he would praise God with a music that had a language
all its own.

The **harp** (*kinnor*) is referred to in Psalm 33:2 as "an instrument of ten strings." It is one of the oldest musical instruments
known (Gen. 4:21). David was skilled in playing it (1 Sam.
16:23). Apparently it was small enough to be carried (1 Sam.
10:5). To play it one plucked the strings.

The poet could express in music feelings for which he had no
words. Indeed, music has a mystical effect on the human spirit.
The heart of God would be gladdened by the strumming of the
harp strings, for they would convey a message of the psalmist's
heart strings that he could not otherwise put into words.

So sing when your heart is heavy, when your pathway is dark. You will be surprised and gratified to see how quickly this will drive away the gloom.

43:5: Why art thou cast down, O my soul? and why art thou disquieted within me? hope in God: for I shall yet praise him, who is the health of my countenance, and my God.

The psalmist closed his psalm with the third repetition of the refrain (42:5,11; 43:5). But this time there is a difference in its tone. First, it was a lament, then an attempt to reassure himself, and, finally, it is a song of praise and assurance.

Cast down literally means "sunk down." He had been sunk in the slough of despondency. **Disquieted within me** means "disturbed within me" (NIV). Now, however, his feet were once again planted on the solid rock of faith in God, so he called on his soul to find its **hope in God.** The psalmist declared, **I shall yet praise him,** and identified God as **my God** and **the health of my countenance.** Today **health** refers to soundness of mind and body. In 1611, when the *King James Version* was translated, *health* was a synonym for *help* and was used in the sense of "deliverance." Compare how the same Hebrew word was translated inconsistently in the refrains in 42:5; 42:11; and 43:5. **The health of my countenance** may be understood as "the help to which my countenance turns." Literally, the phrase is "the acts of salvation of His face" (*yesu'ot panayw*). The psalmist praised God for His saving help or mighty acts of deliverance in the past. The *New International Version,* following a few Hebrew manuscripts, offers the translation "my Savior."

Let each person examine his or her own experience. You either have known, know now, or will come to know deeply distressing circumstances of life. But if you will hold onto your faith, remember the brighter former days, turn your present condition over to God, and put your hope in God, you will know His peace and assurance. God can and does help in times of trouble, and He encourages His people in crises.

WHEN IN NEED OF FORGIVENESS

Basic Passage: Psalm 51
Focal Passage: Psalm 51:1-15

INTRODUCTION

1. "I have sinned." These are three of the most difficult words to utter. Yet it is precisely this confession that opens the floodgates of God's grace and mercy.

2. As we study Psalm 51, we must put ourselves in the writer's place. Our sins may not be the same as his, but we need to confess them to God.

3. This lesson is the evangelism lesson for this quarter.

4. The Central Bible Truth of this lesson is that when we confess our sins to God and turn from them, He forgives us and restores us to a right relationship with Him.

5. The purpose of this lesson is to help you confess any known sin to God and ask for His forgiveness.

6. This lesson seeks to answer the question, How can I be sure God will forgive me for my sins?

I. SOME PRELIMINARY CONSIDERATIONS

1. The Superscription

The superscription to Psalm 51 tells us four things. First, it was part of an earlier collection of psalms–**To the chief Musician.** Second, the type of psalm it is–**A psalm** (*mizmor*), meaning it was sung to the accompaniment of a musical instrument. Third, the authorship–**of David** (*le dawid*). Fourth, the historical background–**when Nathan the prophet came unto him, after he had gone in to Bath-sheba.**

2. The Background

The superscription indicates the background to the psalm. David wrote it following the events described in 2 Samuel 11:1–12:23. David was the most powerful king in the Middle East. He should have been with his army as it laid siege to Rabbah [RAB-uh]. Instead, he "tarried still in Jerusalem" (2 Sam. 11:1).

In the cool of the evening he walked on the flat roof of his palace. From this roof he saw Bathsheba taking a bath. Succumbing to temptation, he sent for her and had sex with her. Did not other oriental rulers do the same? So why not David?

Soon Bathsheba sent word she was pregnant. Thinking he could cover up his sin, David ordered Joab, the commander of his military forces, to send Bathsheba's husband home. If Uriah spent the night with his wife, he would assume the child was his.

Uriah, however, refused to go in to his wife while his fellow soldiers were in the field of battle. He slept in the quarters of David's servants. Seeing his plan had failed, David sent Uriah back to the battle and by him a letter to Joab. Unknown to Uriah, he carried his own death warrant. The king ordered him to be placed in combat, where he was sure to be killed. After Bathsheba's period of mourning for her husband, David married her. In due time, Bathsheba bore David a son.

To his sin of adultery David added the sin of murder. After the child was born, the Lord sent Nathan the prophet to David. Nathan told David a clever parable by which he caused David to see his sins (2 Sam. 12:1-7a). Nathan told David the child would die and David's house would know no peace as long as he lived (2 Sam. 12:7b-14). David was plunged into grief. Probably out of that grief he wrote this psalm.

II. FOCAL PASSAGE EXAMINED (Ps. 51:1-15)

Psalm 51 is a classic statement of repentance and confession and a plea for forgiveness and renewal. Psalm 51 is one of seven penitential psalms (Pss. 6; 32; 38; 51; 102; 130; 143). Nowhere do we see a greater baring of one's soul before God. David was the king of an oriental kingdom, with soldiers and mighty men that did his bidding. But here we see him as a helpless sinner, naked and defenseless, begging God to cleanse him from his sin.

1. The Cry for Forgiveness (Ps. 51:1-2)

In no way did David try to rationalize or justify his double sin. Instead, he cried out to God for forgiveness. No longer did he invoke his position as king to justify his conduct. He stood as a repentant sinner before God.

Verses 1-2: **Have mercy upon me, O God, according to thy loving-kindness: according unto the multitude of thy tender mercies blot out my transgressions. Wash me thoroughly from mine iniquity, and cleanse me from my sin.**

David's sins could not be justified on any basis. So he did what any sinner should do. He began his prayer with a plea for **mercy,** not for justice. The verb **have mercy** (*honneni*) occurs 19 times in the Psalms. The Lord is always the subject. Literally, the plea is "be gracious to me." It reminds us the sinner has no right to God's blessings. Therefore, David appealed to two of the Lord's characteristics: His **loving-kindness,** or "unfailing love" (NIV), is the word *hesed* (God's covenant love); and His **tender mercies,** or "great compassion" (NIV), is the word *rahamim.*

Notice the three words David used for his awful acts. **Transgressions** (*pesha'*) means rebellion, setting oneself against the will and law of God. **Iniquity** (*'awon*) is a collective noun. It refers to that which is crooked, twisted, or warped. The major consequence of iniquity is on the inner person—it renders one guilty before God. **Sin** (*hatta't*) means to miss the mark or target of living by God's character and will. David was guilty of all three.

Notice also what David asked the Lord to do about his sins. **Blot out** refers to God's record of David's conduct. It means to erase. Since God alone had this record, only He could do this.

Wash me thoroughly denotes hard, repeated scrubbing. This was necessary since the guilt ran so deep that his entire being was defiled. **Cleanse me** refers to inner cleansing. David wanted to be clean inside and out.

All people have sinned and need to ask God for forgiveness. When sinners turn to God for forgiveness, they can be confident He loves them and is willing to forgive them and to cleanse them from their guilt.

> There is a fountain filled with blood
>   Drawn from Immanuel's veins;
> And sinners, plunged beneath that flood,
>   Lose all their guilty stains.

(William Cowper, "There Is a Fountain," No. 142, *The Baptist Hymnal*, 1991.)

2. The Confession of Sin (Ps. 51:3-6)

David did not attempt to play down the enormity of his guilt.

Verse 3: **For I acknowledge my transgressions: and my sin is ever before me.**

Nathan had said, "Thou art the man" (2 Sam. 12:7). Now David said, "I am the man." He admitted his rebellion against God. His missing the mark of God's will was ever before him.

To make a public confession of one's sin takes great courage—especially for a king of a nation. Nevertheless, this is always the first step toward forgiveness.

Verses 4-5: **Against thee, thee only, have I sinned, and done this evil in thy sight: that thou mightest be justified when thou speakest, and be clear when thou judgest. Behold, I was shapen in iniquity; and in sin did my mother conceive me.**

When David said, **against thee, thee only, have I sinned,** he was not ignoring the other victims of his awful deeds. He had sinned against Bathsheba. He had sinned doubly against Uriah—once against his marriage in committing adultery with his wife and once against his person in causing his death. He had sinned against the child, against his nation, and against himself. But these paled when compared to his sin against God. For sin–first, last, and always–is against God. Sin violates God's nature, character, will, and law. While sin has its social aspects in that it harms other people–and even the very fabric of society–sin harms God most of all.

David was ready for whatever punishment the Lord might give to him. He declared God blameless–**justified** or "right" (NIV)–in His sentence and righteous–or **clear**–in His judgment. Though David had pleaded for mercy (v. 1), he stood ready to submit to God's judgment.

At the same time, David placed the blame for his sin on no one but himself. He did not seek to justify it as currently acceptable conduct among kings. He made no mention of Bathsheba's part in his sin. When he said, **I was shapen in iniquity; and in sin did my mother conceive me,** he was not making an attempt to excuse himself or to justify his actions. **In sin did my mother conceive me** does not mean his mother sinned when she conceived David in wedlock. This is another way of saying he was born with a tendency toward sin.

Verse 6: **Behold, thou desirest truth in the inward parts: and in the hidden part thou shalt make me to know wisdom.**

David realized that following the desire of his flesh brought him to this low state. He knew God's desire is for **truth**–honesty or loyalty (*'emet*)–**in the inward parts** (*battuhot*) or **in the hidden part** (*satum*), that is, in the inner person. But David also knew he was warped, sinful, and depraved on the inside. Only by receiving God's wisdom–**thou shalt make me to know wisdom**–could David be changed on the inside. As tragic as David's sin was, he had learned from it. There is hope for such a person.

3. The Cleansing from Sin (Ps. 51:7-9)

In his prayer David now began to ask for forgiveness, renewal, and restoration.

Verse 7: **Purge me with hyssop, and I shall be clean: wash me, and I shall be whiter than snow.**

Hyssop probably was sprigs from the marjoram plant that often was used in cleansing and purification ceremonies (Ex. 12:22; Lev. 14:4-6; Num. 19:6-7). Not only did David want to be in God's presence, but he also wanted to be **clean** and thus fit for His presence. He said, **wash me,** so that his soul would be **whiter than** the whiteness of new-fallen **snow.** The vile filthiness of David's present sinful condition stood in stark contrast to the whiteness he longed to have. As James Nicholson wrote:

> Lord Jesus, for this I most humbly entreat;
> I wait, blessed Lord, at Thy crucified feet;
> By faith, for my cleansing I see Thy blood flow:
> Now wash me, and I shall be whiter than snow.
> Whiter than snow, yes, whiter than snow;
> Now wash me, and I shall be whiter than snow.

("Whiter than Snow," No. 325, *The Baptist Hymnal,* 1991.)

Verse 8: **Make me to hear joy and gladness; that the bones which thou hast broken may rejoice.**

God alone could restore heavenly music in David's soul and enable him to experience the ecstasy of **joy** and **gladness.** So crushed was David by his guilt that he felt as if his **bones** had been **broken.** He prayed that these bones might be healed so he could jump for joy in his worship and praise of God.

Verse 9: **Hide thy face from my sins, and blot out all mine iniquities.**

David knew that joy and gladness would return only if God removed his sins. So once again David looked at the enormity of his guilt. Never did he try to play down his sins. This time David prayed that God would **hide thy face from my sins** and **blot out all mine iniquities.** This is another way of asking for forgiveness. For God to **hide** His **face** from sins is the equivalent of putting them out of His presence.

Cleansing from sin is not merely the removal of guilty feelings. Cleansing involves the total removal of the sins that cause

the guilty feelings. Some people want their guilty feelings removed, but they want to continue doing the sinful actions that
caused their guilt in the first place. We need to be honest before
God and seek the removal of all sins from our lives.

4. The Creation of a New Heart (Ps. 51:10-12)

Forgiveness of sins results in restoration to a right relationship with God. David asked God for a pure heart, a steadfast
spirit, the joy of salvation, and a willing spirit. These things
would help him avoid future sins. David wanted to have God
involved in his life.

Verse 10: **Create in me a clean heart, O God; and renew
a right spirit within me.**

Heart is used here in the sense of the whole person. **Create**
refers to an act of God alone. People may mend or repair, but
only God can create. David recognized that outward reforming
of his life was not enough. What he needed was something done
to him from within. His heart needed to be made **clean** or
"pure" (NIV). So, in effect, David asked God to become his Creator all over again.

To his request for a new heart, David also linked a request for
a new spirit. He asked God to **renew a right spirit within me.**
The *New International Version* reads, "renew a steadfast spirit
within me." He wanted to pursue God's way, not go on living in
his own sinful ways.

Verse 11: **Cast me not away from thy presence; and take
not thy holy spirit from me.**

David wanted God's presence away from his sins, but he did
not want to be away from God's **presence.** David was so vile
that he did not belong in God's presence. If he received justice
and not mercy, he would be **cast** out from God's presence. So un-
holy was he that he feared God would snatch His **holy spirit**
from him. If only he had thought of these things before he committed his terrible sins, how much better off he would have been!

The words of verse 11, **take not thy holy spirit from me,** are capitalized differently in the translations. In some versions (such as the NIV, CEV, and NASB), both "Holy" and "Spirit" are capitalized. In the *American Standard Version*, "holy" is not capitalized but "Spirit" is capitalized. In other versions (such as the KJV, NRSV, and REB), neither **holy** nor **spirit** is capitalized–showing the translators did not understand the words as a reference to the third person of the Trinity but to God's presence. In fact, even though the Spirit frequently is mentioned in the Old Testament, the expression **thy holy spirit** is unusual. Only here and in Isaiah 63:10-11 is this terminology used in the Hebrew Masoretic Text. Interestingly, in Isaiah 63 the expression is parallel with "the angel of his presence" in verse 9. Thus these words do not concern eternal security or the issue of whether one can lose his or her salvation. David probably was thinking of the experience of his predecessor, King Saul, whom God cast off because of his misdeeds and from whom God withdrew His spirit (1 Sam. 16:1,7,14).

Verse 12: **Restore unto me the joy of thy salvation; and uphold me with thy free spirit.**

Notice David did not pray for God to **restore** his salvation. Though sinful, David was still God's child. David prayed for God to **restore unto me the** *joy* **of thy** [God's] **salvation** (italics added). David also asked God to **uphold me with thy free spirit.** The *New International Version* translates this "grant me a willing spirit to sustain me." In verse 10 David asked God for a "steadfast spirit" (NIV); here he asked God for a "willing spirit"–that is, a spirit of enthusiasm, a spirit eager to do God's will.

Some people never have experienced the new birth. They need a new heart. Some Christians may feel that because of the severity of their sins, God will withdraw from them. These Christians need to understand that God desires to restore them completely, not abandon them. Many other Christians are unhappy because of their sinful living. These Christians need to learn that only as they live in the will of God will they experience the full joy of God's salvation.

5. The Counsel to Others (Ps. 51:13-15)

Once a person has been saved, the first impulse is to tell others about it. That way they too can have the same experience. This same principle applies when a child of God has experienced forgiveness of some grievous sin. So David vowed to tell other sinners about God's forgiving grace.

Verses 13-15: **Then will I teach transgressors thy ways; and sinners shall be converted unto thee. Deliver me from bloodguiltiness, O God, thou God of my salvation: and my tongue shall sing aloud of thy righteousness. O Lord, open thou my lips; and my mouth shall show forth thy praise.**

Some Christians think they cannot be effective for God because of past failures. How can they talk to others about sin when they have committed the same sins?

Who is better equipped to witness to other **transgressors** than one who has plumbed the depths of sin and by God's grace been lifted to the heights of joy because of sins forgiven? David had known the joy of fellowship with God. He knew the agony of a marred fellowship. He also knew the exhilarating bliss of that fellowship restored. This is why God has entrusted the gospel not to angels but to sinners saved by grace. Through his witness, David saw other **sinners** being **converted** or turning again to God. Thus he prayed, **O Lord, open thou my lips; and my mouth shall show forth thy praise.**

Christians can be motivated by the same desire that motivated David: a desire to see others freed from guilt and to see others experience the same joy and forgiveness they have experienced. For most of us our sins are not those of David; but God does not weigh sins—some heavy, some light. To Him *sin* is *sin*. And sin is rebellion against God. Nevertheless, out of David's agonizing experience we learn how to deal with our sins. Through a broken and contrite heart David received forgiveness (v. 17). So can we! Then he told others about it. So should we!

July 27

WHEN IN NEED OF PROTECTION

Basic Passage: Psalm 91
Focal Passage: Psalm 91:1-16

INTRODUCTION

1. In one way or another, at one time or another, from one danger or another, we all need God's protection.

2. The Central Bible Truth of this lesson is that the Lord will protect His people when they seek refuge in Him.

3. The purpose of this lesson is to help you determine to seek God's protection when you face danger.

4. This lesson seeks to answer the question, How can I cope with danger?

FOCAL PASSAGE EXAMINED (Ps. 91:1-16)

Psalm 91 contains both a wisdom psalm (vv. 1–13) and a divine oracle (vv. 14–16). The psalm is closely connected to Psalms 90 and 92 in language and thought. Psalm 91 is the only one of the three that does not have a superscription.

1. The Refuge (Ps. 91:1-2)

The psalmist began with a general statement in the third person directed to anyone seeking wisdom. In verse 2 he changed to first person and thereby showed his personal appropriation of the general statement in verse 1 before he applied it to his readers.

Verses 1-2: **He that dwelleth in the secret place of the most High shall abide under the shadow of the Almighty. I will say of the Lord, He is my refuge and my fortress: my God; in him will I trust.**

The psalmist found a refuge. To describe his refuge, the psalmist used four divine names for God and four metaphors for His protection in verses 1-2.

Thirty-six times in the Old Testament, always in poetry, God called Himself by the name **the most High** (*'Elyon*). The *King James Version* uses *'elyon* as a descriptive title, not capitalizing the word **most**. The *New International Version,* and most modern translations–including the *New King James Version*–use it as a proper name and capitalize it, "Most High." The name *'elyon* stresses God's supremacy, exaltedness, overwhelming majesty, and omnipotence.

The Almighty (*Shaddai*) appears 48 times in the Old Testament, 31 of which are in the Book of Job. Only two are in the Psalter (here and Ps. 68:14). *Shadday* is the name by which God sustained the homeless patriarchs (Ex. 6:3).

The Lord (*Yahweh*) is the personal covenant name by which God introduced Himself to Moses (Ex. 3:14). This name is called the *Tetragrammaton* (*tetra,* four, and *grammaton,* letters) because it is made up of four Hebrew consonants, YHWH. Translated "LORD" (in small capital letters) or "Jehovah" (ASV), this name for God is the most frequently occurring of His names, being used some 5,321 times and occurring in every book of the Old Testament except Ecclesiastes and Esther. The name Yahweh speaks of God's nearness, concern, and redemptive covenant.

My God (*'elohay,* from *Elohim*) is the general term for God in the Old Testament, occurring some 2,570 times. The first occurrence of the word *Elohim* links it with creation; other occurrences link it with God's sovereignty over creation. Here the term *Elohim* is made more intimate by the possessive **my.**

The four metaphors for security are: **the secret place, the shadow, my refuge,** and **my fortress.** The first two metaphors suggest the imagery of a bird; the second two suggest the imagery of a military stronghold. To **abide** is to "rest" (NIV). What the *King James Version* calls **the secret place** is "the covert" or "shelter" (NIV). **Under the shadow of** may anticipate the metaphor in verse 4 or it may refer to "being under the protection of" the Almighty, suggesting a figure of an Oriental host who offered protection to his guest at the cost of his own life, if necessary.

2. The Reassurance (Ps. 91:3-8)

The psalmist knew he was safe. Regardless of the danger or the degree of the threat, he was assured of God's protection. So he went on to unfold for each of his readers—the **thee** ("you," NIV) is singular throughout—the kinds of safety involved in his refuge. Most of the dangers he named are the kind that strike unseen and against which both the strong and the weak are helpless.

Verses 3-8: **Surely he shall deliver thee from the snare of the fowler, and from the noisome pestilence. He shall cover thee with his feathers, and under his wings shalt thou trust: his truth shall be thy shield and buckler. Thou shalt not be afraid for the terror by night; nor for the arrow that flieth by day; nor for the pestilence that walketh in darkness; nor for the destruction that wasteth at noonday. A thousand shall fall at thy side, and ten thousand at thy right hand; but it shall not come nigh thee. Only with thine eyes shalt thou behold and see the reward of the wicked.**

He is emphatic in verse 3 to emphasize the Lord's care. The Lord is involved in the welfare and protection of His people. **The snare of the fowler** was the virtually invisible net of the bird catcher. This refers to protection from hidden dangers and plots that unexpectedly catch us and entangle us. **The noisome pestilence** means the destroying or "deadly pestilence" (NIV).

Verse 4 shows both God's tender and sufficient care. It begins with a warm fuzzy picture of a protective parent bird who covers her young with her pinions and moves to the hard, unyielding strength of armor. **Under his wings shalt thou trust** is better rendered "under his wings you will find refuge" (NIV).

A missionary told of an experience he had in Angola, Africa. A fire swept through the bush, leaving destruction in its wake. After the fire burned itself out, he was walking along a trail when he spied the charred remains of a mother hen on her nest. He kicked over the burned carcass with the toe of his boot, and to his amazement out from under the body of the mother hen ran some baby chicks. The chicks found refuge under their mother's wings. Under her wings, the fire that swept over her did not touch them.

In Matthew 23:37 and Luke 13:34 Jesus addressed the residents of Jerusalem and likened Himself to a mother hen who wished to gather her chicks under her wings to protect them—but they refused. Oh, how different is the experience of believers that William Cushing captured when he wrote his hymn "Under His Wings":

> Under His wings I am safely abiding.
>   Tho' the night deepens and tempests are wild,
> Still I can trust Him; I know He will keep me.
>   He has redeemed me, and I am His child.
>
> Under His wings, oh, what precious enjoyment!
>   There will I hide till life's trials are o'er;
> Sheltered, protected, no evil can harm me.
>   Resting in Jesus, I'm safe evermore.
>
> Under His wings, under His wings,
>   Who from His love can sever?
> Under His wings my soul shall abide,
>   Safely abide forever.

His truth is better rendered "his faithfulness" (NIV). The image of **shield and buckler** develops the metaphor of the refuge and fortress from verse 2, but the exact meaning is open to three interpretations because of the term **buckler,** which is used only here in the Scripture. (The technical term for a word used only one time is a *hapax legomenon.*) The word translated **buckler** (*soherah*) is derived from a root involving "circle" or "circumference." In the Jewish Targum, the *King James Version,* the *Revised Standard Version,* and the *New Revised Standard*

Version, the **buckler** was understood to refer to a round shield. Kidner also claimed the **shield** referred to the large and static protection and the **buckler** to the small and mobile protection (*Psalms 73–150,* 333). Another possibility, following a Syriac root for a walled enclosure, is reflected in the *New American Standard Bible,* which has "bulwark," and the *New International Version,* which has "rampart." A third possibility is that of Marvin E. Tate, who saw the two as a *hendiadys* (Tate, "Psalms 51–100," 448). A *hendiadys* (literally meaning "one through two") is the expression of one idea by two nouns usually connected by "and." Tate rendered it, "shield of protection."

The dangers in verses 5-6 are fourfold and alternate between darkness and light: (1) **terror by night,** (2) **the arrow that flieth by day,** (3) **the pestilence that walketh in darkness,** and (4) **the destruction that wasteth at noonday.**

Midnight and **noonday** were times of special anxiety for the Hebrews. One is more terrified at **night** because things seem more frightening in the dark and because enemies often attack at night. The word for **terror** (*pahad*) is a strong verb for fear. It stresses the immediacy of the object of fear or the resulting quaking and trembling. **The arrow that flieth by day** may refer to an enemy's attack or to sunstroke. **Pestilence** and **the destruction that wasteth** may refer to the "plague that destroys" (NIV).

Some interpreters think verse 5 refers to dangers from other people in war and verse 6 refers to dangers from diseases, epidemics, and plagues. That is, verse 5 refers to dangers from persons; verse 6 refers to dangers from pestilence.

These distinctions–night and day, natural and human–should not be pressed too hard however. By referring to dangers that could occur in the day or night, the psalmist probably was saying they could occur at any time. A standard figure of speech in which something is divided into two parts to characterize the whole (such as saying "heaven and earth" to mean "all creation") is called a *merismus.* The psalmist was making a comprehensive statement about the perils of life (Tate, "Psalms 51–100," 454).

The Lord's protective care is not limited to certain times or places. He gives protection constantly, by day and by night.

In the statement **a thousand shall fall at thy side, and ten thousand at thy right hand; but it shall not come nigh thee,** the word **thee** is emphatic: "to you it will not draw near." What **it** refers to is unclear. **It** may refer to the plague or scourge of verse 6, or **it** may be an indefinite subject that refers to whatever caused the thousands to fall.

These statements do not mean that harm will never come to God's children. In other words, this is not what necessarily will happen; it is what God can bring to pass. God is able to defend His own in what seem to be situations of inescapable dangers. But this is not a blanket immunity against adversity. As Kidner pointed out, Romans 8:28 does not exclude verse 35 and Luke 21:16 does not void the paradox of verse 18 (*Psalms 73–150,* 333).

The reward of the wicked is "the punishment of the wicked" (NIV). When the godly are delivered, they often see how the wicked are paid back in full for their wickedness. As H. C. Leupold reminded us, "God's faithfulness reckons with both the godly and the ungodly" (*Exposition of Psalms,* 654).

The statements of verses 3-8 ensure two things: (1) nothing can touch God's people except by His permission, and (2) the wicked will not escape God's retribution (Kidner, *Psalms 73–150,* 333). This should help us as we encounter multiple threats and dangers in our world. In the face of these dangers, when we are in need of protection, we can be confident of God's faithful presence, care, and strength.

3. The Rescue (Ps. 91:9-13)

God is the guardian of His people and is able to rescue us from any situation we may encounter.

Verses 9-13: **Because thou hast made the Lord, which is my refuge, even the most High, thy habitation; there shall no evil befall thee, neither shall any plague come nigh**

thy dwelling. For he shall give his angels charge over thee, to keep thee in all thy ways. They shall bear thee up in their hands, lest thou dash thy foot against a stone. Thou shalt tread upon the lion and adder: the young lion and the dragon shalt thou trample under feet.

Verse 9 is difficult to translate and interpret. One problem is that it is unclear to whom the emphatic **thou** ("you," NIV) refers. Another difficulty concerns the alternation between the third person and the first person. Many modern translations emend the text to avoid the first person of **my refuge.** For example, the *New Revised Standard Version* reads, "Because you have made the Lord *your refuge,* the Most High your dwelling place, no evil shall befall you" (italics added). The *New International Version* agrees with the *King James Version* in retaining the first person–albeit in a clause set off by dashes–but changes the **because** (*ki*) to "if you make": "If you make the Most High your dwelling–even the Lord, who is my refuge–then no harm will befall you."

Evil means "harm" (NIV), **plague** means "disaster" (NIV), and **dwelling** literally is "tent" (NIV) in verse 10. The negatives of verse 10 (**no evil . . . neither . . . any plague**) have their complement in the positive declaration that God **shall give his angels charge over thee, to keep thee in all thy ways** in verse 11. **Ways** refers to the activities and conduct of one's life, that is, the "ways of life," not merely to one's journeys. **To keep** means "to guard" (NIV). To **bear thee up in their hands** indicates special care and support. To **dash thy foot against a stone** indicates stumbling and is a frequent metaphor for trouble and misfortune in the Psalms (37:31; 38:16; 56:13; 73:2; 94:18; 116:8).

The Bible teaches that angels protect people from harm (Gen. 24:7; Pss. 34:7; 103:20-21; Isa. 63:9; Heb. 1:14), but verses 11-12 touch on a topic that has become popular in recent years, even among those who do not believe the Bible–guardian angels. Psalm 91 testifies to their existence but gives little detail about how they operate on our behalf. Surely the biblical text does not go as far as the Jewish Talmud, which teaches that two ministering angels accompany a person through life and testify about that person's conduct at the judgment after death. Interestingly, Satan quoted the promise of verses 11-12 out of context in tempting Jesus (Matt. 4:6; Luke 4:10-11). At any rate, the emphasis in these verses is not on the angels but on God; it is **he** [who] **shall give his angels charge over thee.**

Verse 13 moves from the images of the need for help and protection to an image of victorious subjugation that shows God's people are not merely survivors but victors. The translations, however, differ on the creatures named in verse 13. There are three main views, the confusion mainly being over what is meant by the first of the four creatures named (the *shahal*) and whether that term affects the meaning of the third term (the *kepir*).

The *King James Version* understands the four terms as two parallel statements: **the lion and adder** and **the young lion and the dragon.** The Hebrew word for **dragon** (*tannin*) can refer to anything from large snakes to enormous sea creatures. In some contexts, the word refers to a sea dragon or sea serpent. The *New American Bible,* a Roman Catholic version, retains "dragon." Rotherham, in *The Emphasized Bible,* has "crocodile." In Exodus 7:9,12 and Deuteronomy 32:33 the word clearly refers to a snake. Thus, the *New International Version,* the *New American Standard Bible,* and the *New Revised Standard Version* substitute "serpent" for **dragon.** All three of these modern translations agree with the *King James Version* and understand the sequence as lion-snake, lion-snake. The *New International Version* offers "the great lion" for **the young lion** (*kepir*). *Kepir* is one of the Hebrew words for a lion, but it is uncertain whether this word specifies the lion's age or prowess. The *New International Version* and *New American Standard Bible* read "the cobra" for **adder** (*peten*). However, since the cobra does not appear in Palestine, the *New Revised Standard Version* is correct to retain "the adder."

Durham (BBC, "Psalms," 359) represented a second view. He acknowledged that *shahal* and *kepir* normally mean a lion and a young lion respectively. He then stated, "but it hardly makes sense to speak of stepping on and trampling down a lion, even a young one." Based on this assumption and on the belief that the two terms *shahal* and *kepir* are parallel and thus must refer to the same animal, Durham interpreted *kepir* (young lion)–about which there really is no question concerning its meaning–in light of *shahal*. He took both terms in a reptilian sense. Durham wrote, "It is only logical that some sort of dangerous reptile is meant, perhaps by figurative language whose meaning is now lost." The *Revised English Bible* (and its predecessor, the *New English Bible*), following the Septuagint and the Syriac, also represents this position, translating all four terms in verse 13 as references to snakes: "You will tread on asp and cobra, you will trample on snake and serpent" (REB).

A third possibility is to take the first of the terms (*shahal*) in a reptilian sense and to reject the parallelism with the third term (*kepir*). This allows for the third term to be rendered in its normal sense of lion. The *New American Bible* represents this interpretation: "You shall tread upon the asp and the viper; you shall trample down the lion and the dragon." So does James Moffatt's *A New Translation of the Bible*: "you can walk over reptiles and cobras, trampling on lions and on dragons."

Depending on their identification of the four creatures, some interpreters want to see an open, devouring danger versus a cunning, underhanded dealing. On the other hand, both lions and snakes attack with little warning and from hidden places. The point simply may be that both ambush their victims. Such creatures frequently are symbols for evil men and powers that oppose God's people and from which He rescues them (Deut. 32:33; Ps. 58:3-6).

4. The Result (Ps. 91:14-16)

In verses 14-16 God speaks; it is His oracle. The *New International Version* makes this clear by adding "says the Lord" in verse 14. We should gain confidence from the fact that the last word is spoken by God–not by us.

Verses 14-16: **Because he hath set his love upon me, therefore will I deliver him: I will set him on high, because he hath known my name. He shall call upon me, and I will answer him: I will be with him in trouble; I will deliver him, and honor him. With long life will I satisfy him, and show him my salvation.**

The Lord cited three reasons why He acts on behalf of the one who trusts in Him, and then He gave eight examples of His safekeeping. First, **because he hath set his love upon me.** To **set** one's **love upon** someone is to set one's heart on someone. **Love** (*hashaq*) refers to a deep longing or desire to cling to, to be attached to, or to be joined together with someone. This is the love that will not let go. The expression is used of a person cleaving in love to another person (Gen. 34:8; Deut. 21:11), of the Lord's devotion to Israel (Deut. 7:7-8; 10:15), and of the Lord's love for His own (Isa. 38:17); but nowhere else is it used of a person's devotion to God. The second reason is **because he hath known my name.** This reason stresses revelation, but **known my name** refers to more than mere information. Someone's **name** stands for the person's character. Thus this refers to a personal acquaintance with the God whose character is revealed in His name; it is to have a close personal relationship with Him (Ps. 9:2,10). The *New International Version* reads, "for he acknowledges my name." Third, **he shall call upon me.** This indicates that one knows who is the Helper and who is the helpless; it is a **call** for grace.

God's safekeeping of the person who loves Him is centered around eight actions. Possibly these verbs show progression or move to an ascending climax. What God said **I will** do was (1) **deliver him,** (2) **set him on high,** (3) **answer him,** (4) **be with him,** (5) **deliver him,** (6) **honor him,** (7) **satisfy him** (with long life), and (8) **show him my salvation.** Two different words for **deliver** are used in verses 14 and 15. The Hebrew word in verse 14 is *palat.* It is used 27 times in the Old Testament, 19 of which are in the Psalter. Usually, the psalmists either addressed the word to God in the imperative as they sought God's deliverance, or they used the verb in a testimony of praise for God's deliverance. This is the only time God is the subject of the verb. The *New International Version* renders it "rescue." The other Hebrew word for **deliver** in verse 15 is *halas*. It is used with the meaning "rescue" 16 times, but only in the poetic material in Job, Psalms, and Proverbs. The *New American Standard Bible* and the *New Revised Standard Version* render this word "rescue."

To **set him on high** means "to make him inaccessibly high" (Ps. 69:29). It refers to being put out of the way of harm. The *New International Version* reads, "I will protect him." When God promised He would **be with him in trouble,** He promised to be there with him in hard times, in times of distress. It is unusual for God to **honor** a human being–but notice the promise in 1 Samuel 2:30! When He does so, He brings the person dignity and success.

God promised to **satisfy him** (*sabea*) or give him the fullness of **long life. With long life** literally is "with extended number of days." Elsewhere God is said to reward His people with "length of days" in this life (Ex. 20:12 and Deut. 5:16 [the Fourth Commandment]; Ex. 23:26; Deut. 30:20; Ps. 21:4; Prov. 3:2,16; Eph. 6:3).

Finally, God promised to **show him my salvation** (*yesu'ah*). This promise may mean God would "let him see my saving care" (Moffatt) or "my saving power" (CEV). On the other hand, it may be a reference to God's future eschatological salvation. Psalm 149:4 tells us, "The Lord taketh pleasure in his people: he will beautify the meek with salvation." H. C. Leupold (*Exposition of Psalms,* 656) wrote, "But the summarizing statement–'and show him My salvation'–makes this one gift stand out with particular clarity. Since 'salvation' is a term of such breadth as to include every possible form of deliverance, physical and spiritual, the statement amounts to this: 'I will give my own true followers so many proofs of the help that I bestow upon them that the one fact that will impress them above all others is: how wonderfully God can deliver in all needs of body and soul!'"

This assurance, however, is only addressed to the ones who love, or are devoted, to the Lord–to those who cling to Him.

UNIT III: *Issues Facing Society*

August 3

OLD AGE

Basic Passages: 1 Timothy 5:1-10,16; Titus 2:1-5
Focal Passages: 1 Timothy 5:1-10,16; Titus 2:1-5

INTRODUCTION

1. Today's lesson begins a five-session unit on "Issues Facing Society." This unit addresses the topics of old age, money, prejudice, violence, and alcohol and drugs.

2. The Central Bible Truth of this lesson is that older adults deserve respect and assistance when they need it and are to involve themselves in ministry as they continue to age.

3. The purpose of this lesson is to help you, as a younger adult, discover ways you will express respect, encouragement, or assistance when needed to an older adult; or to help you, as an older adult, discover ways you can continue to involve yourself in ministry.

4. This lesson seeks to answer the questions, What are my responsibilities toward older adults? How can I, as an older adult, continue to minister?

I. SOME PRELIMINARY CONSIDERATIONS

1. The Background

In A.D. 61-63 Paul experienced what is known as his first Roman imprisonment. During that time he wrote the Prison Epistles: Ephesians, Philippians, Colossians, and Philemon. From A.D. 63-66 Paul was free from prison and engaged in missionary work. He evidently went to Spain (see Rom. 15:24) and then back across the Mediterranean to Ephesus. In A.D. 65 he wrote to his associate Timothy, probably from Macedonia, whom he had left in charge of the Christian work in and around Ephesus.

With Paul, Titus went to Crete to begin a Christian work. Paul left Titus there to solidify the work. Later Paul wrote his letter to Titus, probably from Nicopolis [nih-KAHP-oh-liss] in A.D. 66. At Nicopolis Paul was arrested and taken back to Rome, where eventually he was beheaded. Titus was the next to the last letter Paul wrote, followed only by 2 Timothy. These three letters, 1 and 2 Timothy and Titus, are called the Pastorals or Pastoral Epistles based on their content.

2. Old Age

Today's society is an aging population. Demographics point to the "graying of America." No society has ever had such a large proportion of its members reaching senior adulthood at the same time as ours. This phenomenon has massive implications for the health-care and health-services industries. At the same time, contemporary society emphasizes youth, functional values, and contribution capability. The once-honored elderly are now seen as limited in their functional capability and in their ability to make a contribution to society. They are viewed as a liability and a drain on the social resources. Hence, they often are neglected, pushed aside, and scorned. Sometimes they even are physically abused or killed. The Bible teaches that older adults are to be respected and assisted when they need it, and that they are to continue to find ways to involve themselves in ministry.

Robert Browning (Ely, *I Quote,* 5) wrote about aging:
>Grow old along with me!
>The best is yet to be,
>The last of life, for which the first was made.
>Our times are in His hand,
>Who saith: "A whole I planned,
>Youth shows but half; trust God; see all, nor be afraid."

II. FOCAL PASSAGES EXAMINED
(1 Tim. 5:1-10,16; Titus 2:1-5)

Although this lesson's focal verses primarily deal with older women and widows, the teachings can be applied to ministering to all older adults and to the ministry opportunities for all older adults.

1. Respect for Older People (1 Tim. 5:1-2)

In 1 Timothy 5 Paul gave Timothy practical advice about how to deal with people and problems within the church fellowship. He began by showing the attitude Timothy should have toward various age groups—respect.

1 Tim. 5:1-2: **Rebuke not an elder, but entreat him as a father; and the younger men as brethren. The elder women as mothers; the younger as sisters, with all purity.**

Paul viewed the church as a family. In the Greek the emphasis is on age, as shown in each statement beginning with an age designation. For instance, **rebuke not an elder** literally is "an elder do not rebuke." Here **elder** clearly refers to an older man, not to the office of elder as in verses 17 and 19. The verb rendered **rebuke** basically means "to strike upon," as with the fists. But here the idea refers to speaking to older people with harsh words. As a comparatively young man, Timothy was to respect older people. Rather than speak to an older man harshly, he should **entreat,** beseech, "exhort" (NIV), or plead with him as though he were his **father. Elder women** renders the feminine form of the word for **elder** in verse 1. Timothy should respect and reverence such a one as though she were his own **mother.** This instruction reflects the general attitude of reverence for one's parents.

Similarly, Timothy was to regard **younger men** as brothers and **the younger** women **as sisters.** Here **brethren** and **sisters** refers to biological rather than religious relationships. Thus, "Treat younger men as you would your own brother. . . . Show the same respect to younger women that you would to your sister" (CEV). The word for **purity** (*hagneia*) is akin to the word for "holy" and appears only here and in 4:12 in the New Testament. *The Living Bible* translates **with all purity** as "thinking only pure thoughts about them."

Believers are to treat all people with respect. But when younger believers treat older members of the church with the respect they deserve, the church becomes a model of the way God intends for society to treat older people.

Elderly people respond favorably to kind attention; they respond negatively to a lack of it. Often elderly people are lonely. They feel others regard them as being in the way. For many years some churches majored on programs for youth to the neglect of their older adults. Happily, many churches now have activities designed for older adults and ministries in which older adults can be involved. It is a good thing, since with modern medical skill people are living longer. The retired group increases regularly. They should not be coddled but used where their abilities and health permit. There are many things older adults can do for the Lord.

2. Ministry to Older People (1 Tim. 5:3-10,16)

In Judaism, care for the elderly was traditional. This practice carried over into Christianity. According to Cornelius of Rome, by the middle of the third century there were 1,500 widows and needy on the Roman church's dole (Eusebius, *Ecclesiastical History*, 6:43). This particular case concerns the care of elderly widows. Apparently in Ephesus, as in Jerusalem (Acts 6:1), the care of widows created problems in the church. So Paul told Timothy how to deal with them. First, Paul laid down a principle. Next, he discussed family support. After that, he talked about qualifications for church support. Finally, he stated a disqualification. Some verses are grouped together in this section to make these points clear.

1 Tim. 5:3: **Honor widows that are widows indeed.**

In verse 3 Paul laid down the principle. **Honor** here means not only "to show proper respect for" but also includes "giving financial aid to." Paul used the phrase **widows that are widows indeed** three times (vv. 3,5,16) to stress the responsibility to "those widows who are really in need" (NIV), that is, to widows who had no other means of support. A woman might be bereft of her husband and yet not be in need of financial help from her family or from her church for the necessities of life. Thus the emphasis of this section is on those who need help from others to survive.

1 Tim. 5:4,8,16: **But if any widow have children or nephews, let them learn first to show piety at home, and to requite their parents: for that is good and acceptable before God. . . . But if any provide not for his own, and specially for those of his own house, he hath denied the faith, and is worse than an infidel. . . . If any man or woman that believeth have widows, let them relieve them, and let not the church be charged; that it may relieve them that are widows indeed.**

Widows' families—or in other cases, needy older persons' families—have the first responsibility to provide care and financial support for them. **Nephews** should read "grandchildren" (NIV). In the *King James Version* the word *nephew* always is used in what is now an obsolete sense. In 1611 *nephew* meant "a descendant," and commonly was used of "a grandchild." Thus the **children** and grandchildren are to accept their responsibility toward their progenitors.

Paul cited three reasons for this obligation in verse 4. First, such help is a sign of true piety. **At home** literally reads "to their own household." Of the words **let them learn first to show piety at home,** A. T. Robertson (*Word Pictures in the New Testament,* vol. 4 [Nashville: Broadman Press, 1931], 584) said, "No acts of **piety** toward God will make up for impiety towards parents." Second, this support and care is a form of repayment owed to parents. **Requite** means to pay back. The Greek phrase really means to pay back like for like. Parents looked after their children when the children were young and helpless. Children should do the same for parents when the parents become old and helpless. Paul added a third reason, stating that this is "pleasing to God" (NIV) or **acceptable before God**–a reference to the Fifth Commandment (Ex. 20:12).

In verse 8 Paul reinforced his words from verse 4. He said that **if any provide not for his own, and specially for those of his own house, he hath denied the faith, and is worse than an infidel.** Failure to financially care for the elderly members of one's own household is a denial of the Christian faith. The person who neglects this responsibility is worse than **an infidel** or unbeliever, for even a pagan looks after his own. Thus Paul concluded in verse 16: **If any man or woman that believeth have widows** [in their family], **let them relieve them** [financially assist, help], **and let not the church be charged** ["burdened," NIV]; **that it may relieve** [financially assist, help] **them that are widows indeed** ["those widows who are really in need," NIV].

Paul then gave instructions concerning those widows who had no one else at home to take care of them. These widows the church was obligated to minister to–but only if they met certain conditions. They not only had to be in need; they also had to be faithful Christians in the church and to be Christlike examples before the world.

1 Tim. 5:5,9-10: **Now she that is a widow indeed, and desolate, trusteth in God, and continueth in supplications and prayers night and day. . . . Let not a widow be taken into the number under threescore years old, having been the wife of one man, well reported of for good works; if she have brought up children, if she have lodged strangers, if she have washed the saints' feet, if she have relieved the afflicted, if she have diligently followed every good work.**

In verse 5 Paul described the **widow indeed,** the widow without any visible means of support, with three phrases. First, she was **desolate. Desolate** means that she was "left all alone" (NIV). She was without husband, children, grandchildren, or other near relatives who could help support her. The perfect tense of the participle expresses complete desolation. Second, she **trusteth in God.** In the Greek text this is a perfect tense showing she completely "puts her hope in God" (NIV) and continued to do so. Third, she was a woman of prayer. **In supplications and prayers night and day** means she asked God for help "by night and by day." Paul did not say that she prayed all night and all day. The figure is that she had placed her hope in God and prayed that He would provide for her needs.

The widow whom the church helped support had to meet three qualifications to be **taken into the number** or "put on the list" (NIV) of those supported. First, she could not be **under threescore years old.** Presumably a woman under 60 years old would either be able to work to support herself or would remarry.

Second, the widow was to have been **the wife of one man.** This expression, which is parallel to the requirements for an elder and deacon (3:2,12), either means that (1) she could have been married only one time–thus assuming that if she had been married more than once she would have inherited enough from her husbands to live on–or that (2) she had been "faithful to her husband" (NIV) during her marriage. Thomas D. Lea ("1, 2 Timothy," in *The New American Commentary,* vol. 34 [Nashville: Broadman Press, 1992], 150) represents the view adopted by the *New International Version.* He wrote, "The demand was for lifetime fidelity and not singleness during the remainder of her lifetime."

Third, she was to have been **well reported of for good works.** Paul listed some of the good deeds. The words **if she have diligently followed every good work** show that the list of deeds of mercy and kindness is not exhaustive, nor is it a definitive list of requirements; it is merely representative of the types of actions she already should have performed. The list includes having **brought up children, lodged strangers, washed the saints' feet,** and **relieved the afflicted.** Of these examples, the first was not intended to exclude childless widows from receiving help. The second referred to the practice of hospitality, especially toward traveling Christians and missionaries (Rom. 12:13; 3 John

5-8; 1 Pet. 4:9). The third, washing the saints' feet, may have included the literal practice (Luke 7:44; John 13:14) or simply indicate a humble spirit of service. "Helping those in trouble" (NIV)
may refer to assisting others who were in need or sick, but it may
refer specifically to assisting persecuted believers.

There are other persons, however, whom the church has no
obligation to help financially. Even some widows are unworthy
of the church's help.

**1 Tim. 5:6-7: But she that liveth in pleasure is dead
while she liveth. And these things give in charge, that
they may be blameless.**

The merry widow, probably among the younger widows (see
vv. 11-15), does not deserve financial support from the church.
She is the one who **liveth in pleasure.** Weymouth called her a
"pleasure-loving widow." Other versions describe her as "a widow
given to self-indulgence" (REB), "one who lives voluptuously"
(Berkeley), "she who lives in wantonness" (Montgomery), "she
who gives herself to wanton pleasure" (NASB), "the widow who
plunges into dissipation" (Moffatt), "a widow who gives herself
up to luxury" (Williams), and "a widow who thinks only about
having a good time" (CEV). The conduct of these widows showed
they were not Christians. Such a widow was spiritually **dead
while she liveth.** Obviously such a person does not qualify for
financial assistance from the church. To give money to her would
be a waste of the church's limited resources. Churches need to
know whether those to whom they give money are truly in need
because some people use the church for their own ends.
Churches, as well as individual believers, are to be good stewards of their resources.

The Greek text of verse 7 is unclear whether the instructions
were a warning to the congregation or to the widows. The *New
International Version* assumes the former: "Give the people
these instructions, too, so that no one may be open to blame." So
does the *Contemporary English Version*: "Tell all of this to everyone, so they will do the right thing." The *Revised English Bible,*

however, understands it as a warning to the widows: "Add these instructions to the rest, so that the widows may be above reproach." This is also the opinion of Thomas D. Lea in *The New American Commentary* ("1,2 Timothy," 148).

As in the days of the early church, so it is in our day. The church needs to implement practical ways to provide significant ministry to the elderly who are alone and in need.

3. Ministry of Older People (Titus 2:1-5)

Paul exhorted Titus about his work in Crete.

Titus 2:1: **But speak thou the things which become sound doctrine.**

In the Greek, **thou** (*su*) opens the sentence and thus is emphatic, contrasting Titus with the false teachers of 1:10-16. Titus was commanded to "keep on speaking" (present tense, imperative mood) **the things which become sound doctrine.** The word for **sound** (*hygiainouse*) means "healthy." We get our word *hygiene* from this Greek term.

Paul then gave Titus sound teaching for five specific groups in the church, whom he designated by age, sex, and social position in verses 1-10 (older men, v. 2; older women, v. 3; younger women, vv. 4-5; younger men, vv. 6-8; and slaves, vv. 9-10). In the process Paul taught that older men and older women can be involved in ministry by being examples in faith and practice and by teaching younger believers how to live the Christian life.

Titus 2:2: **That the aged men be sober, grave, temperate, sound in faith, in charity, in patience.**

First, then, Paul indicated the kind of examples older men are to be as spiritual mentors.

The word for **aged men** is *presbytas,* a kindred but different word from *presbyteros* that is used for the church leader or "elder" in 1:5. Paul looked to older men to set the right example for younger men to follow. He named specific things that should characterize them. The word the *King James Version* and *Revised English Bible* translate as **sober** (*nephalious*), many other modern versions translate as "temperate" (NIV, NASB, NRSV). If Paul meant the word literally, then he was forbidding drunkenness. If he meant it figuratively, then he was referring to clarity of mind and good judgment.

Grave (*semnous*) means "sensible" or "dignified" (NASB, REB), as opposed to frivolous or silly. The word describes one's manner of behaving. The *New International Version* translates it "worthy of respect." The *New Revised Standard Version* has "prudent."

The word the *King James Version* and the *Revised English Bible* translate as **temperate** (*sophronas*) means "self-controlled" (NIV). The *New American Standard Bible* translates it "sensible." Actually, this quality is to characterize not only the older men (v. 2) but the older women (**they may teach**, v. 4, is this same Greek word), the younger women (v. 5), and the younger men (v. 6).

Older men also are to be **sound** (healthy; *hygiainontas*) **in faith, in charity, in patience. Faith** has the definite article before it, which normally would indicate "the faith" refers to the body of Christian doctrine. However, each of the three terms has the definite article in front of it. Thus this refers to the older adult's personal faith, personal **charity** or "love" (NIV; *agape*), and personal **patience** (*hupomone*).

The last term—which may be rendered "perseverance" (NASB), "endurance" (NIV, NRSV), "fortitude" (REB), or "steadfastness"—is especially appropriate for older men. "The latter years of life, especially for men, can be filled with regrets, a sense of uselessness or worthlessness, feelings of despair, self-absorption, or even a tendency to relax moral standards because of old age" (Hayne P. Griffin, Jr., "Titus," in *The New American Commentary*, 298).

Titus 2:3: The aged women likewise, that they be in behavior as becometh holiness, not false accusers, not given to much wine, teachers of good things.

Next Paul detailed the kind of examples older women are to be as spiritual mentors. **Aged women** (*presbytidas*) renders the feminine form of the word for "aged men." **In behavior** (*katastemati*) means "in the way they live" (NIV). The term indicates the outward expression of their inner character. The word translated **holiness** or "reverent" (NIV) is used only here in the New Testament. The Greek term (*hieroprepeis*) is made up of the word "temple" (*hieron*) and "fitting" or "appropriate" (*prepeis*). Paul may have coined this term to suggest that older women's conduct or "way of life" should be reflective of a priestess engaged in sacred duties in God's temple. **False accusers** or "slanderers" (NIV) translates *diabolous*. *Diabolos* is the word for *devil,* meaning *slanderer.* All slander is of the devil! **Given to much wine** (see also 1 Tim. 3:3,8; Titus 1:7) literally reads "not enslaved to much wine" (*dedoulomenas,* a perfect passive participle of *douloo,* the verb form of *doulos*–a slave). Possibly, being "addicted to much wine" (NIV) or "slaves to excessive drinking" (REB) was a problem among the Cretan women. Finally, the older women should be **teachers of good things.** This expression renders one Greek word (*kalodidaskalous*; *kalos,* good or beautiful, and *didaskalos,* teacher). The term does not specify formal teaching but indicates advising and encouraging by word and example.

"As children grow up and leave home, the older woman's focus may become less defined as her familial responsibilities become less demanding. This may contribute to feelings of uselessness, loneliness, low self-esteem, and self-pity. Paul suggested in this passage that older women should possess personal godliness, be worthy of respect, and play an essential role in the lives of the younger women in the church" (Griffin, "Titus," NAC, 299).

Titus 2:4-5: **That they may teach the young women to be sober, to love their husbands, to love their children, to be discreet, chaste, keepers at home, good, obedient to their own husbands, that the word of God be not blasphemed.**

Finally Paul identified the kind of teaching older adults can do. The women's roles are mentioned in verses 4-5 and the men's in verses 6-8.

That (*hina*) introduces a purpose clause. Older women are to be **teachers of good things** so that **they may teach the young women. May teach . . . to be sober** (*sophronizosin*) is the verb form of the adjective *sophronas* in verse 2 that means "self-controlled" or "sensible." The verb, which is used only here in the New Testament, means "to make sane," "to bring to their senses," or "to school in the lessons of sobriety and self-control."

Paul then used seven adjectives to indicate what the older women were to teach the younger women. Four of the seven items relate to the home and family. Some translations treat the adjectives independently (KJV, NASB, NRSV); other translations pair some of them (NIV, REB, RSV, NEB).

The first two items are at the heart of a Christian home. **Love their husbands** translates one word (*philandrous*). *Philos* is warm personal love or devotedness. *Andros* comes from *aner*, which may mean *man* or *husband* according to the context. Here it definitely means "lovers of their own husbands," not "lovers of men"! Paul also used just one word to tell the younger women they were to **love their children** (*philoteknous*) with a warm, personal love. **Discreet** is the recurring word *sophronas* that means "self-controlled" (NIV). **Chaste** (*hagnas*) or "pure" (NIV) expresses concern for marital fidelity as well as purity of mind and conduct. **Keepers at home** (*oikourous*) is based on an inferior Greek text. The better reading is "to be busy at home" (NIV; *oikourgous*) and refers to the innumerable duties and responsibilities of managing and taking care of a home. The *New King James Version* reads "homemakers." **Good** (*agathas*) or "kind" (NIV) refers to doing what is beneficial to others. Linked closely with the previous term, it may "indicate a lack of irritability in light of the nagging demands of mundane and routine household duties" (Griffin, "Titus," NAC, 301) or it may simply mean "fulfilling household duties well."

The final item, **obedient to their own husbands,** needs two clarifications. First, the Greek word translated **obedient** (*hypotassomenas*) means "be subject to" (NIV) rather than "to obey."

The Greek word regularly is used in the New Testament regarding the relationship between a husband and a wife (Eph. 5:24; Col. 3:18; 1 Pet. 3:1,5) to focus on God's order of things in the home and the responsible acceptance of it as a Christian obligation by seeking to fulfill the duties that order imposes on one.

Second, the *New International Version* and the *New Revised Standard Version* omit the word **own** (*idiois*), which is in the Greek text, before **husbands** (both here and in the identical expression in 1 Pet. 3:1). This word ensures that the wife's subordination clearly is one of function in her home and that it is between the wife and her husband, not an issue of innate inferiority of women to men in general.

Paul's reason for urging not only the wife's obedience but all seven of these items was **that the word of God be not blasphemed** ("dishonored," NASB). To blaspheme something is to "speak insults against," to "malign" (NIV), or to "discredit" (NRSV) it. The *Revised English Bible* reads, "Then the gospel will not be brought into disrepute." Three times in this chapter Paul emphasized that how Christians live makes an impression on onlookers (vv. 5,8,10). "Proper Christian behavior has a significant impact on pagan attitudes toward Christianity (v. 5), silencing opponents by correct Christian teaching (v. 8), and attracting a lost world to Christianity (v. 10), thus affecting the entire missionary enterprise of the church" (Griffin, "Titus," NAC, 296).

Older adults have a viable and vital ministry within the body of Christ. They may have slowed down in many respects, but they still can teach and train younger Christians from their own growth, experience, and walk with Christ.

As older women can set the example for younger women, so older men may do so for younger men (vv. 6-8). Thus older adults have a responsibility out of their own experience to lead younger adults into a rich Christian family life. It is a heritage to pass on to those who are coming after them. The present-day family greatly needs such help. Those who have traveled the road can make it easier for those who come after them.

August 10

MONEY

Basic Passage: 1 Timothy 6:6-12,17-19
Focal Passages: 1 Timothy 6:6-12,17-19

INTRODUCTION

1. We tend to become like that which we value the most. Tell me your priorities, and I will tell you the kind of person you are.

2. The Central Bible Truth of this lesson is that God, not money, is to be our Master; and we are to use our money to serve His purposes.

3. The purpose of this lesson is to help you decide to use your money more effectively in God's service.

4. This lesson seeks to answer the question, What should I do with my money?

I. SOME PRELIMINARY CONSIDERATIONS

1. A Common Problem

Most adults seem to have the same problem when it comes to money–not enough of it. Many adults live from paycheck to paycheck, barely staying ahead of the bill collectors. Some people hoard their financial resources, storing them up in stocks, bonds, and large bank accounts. Others spend their money only on themselves. When it comes to money, some people are needy; others are greedy; many are both!

2. A Word from the Wise

Matthew Henry wrote, "There is a burden of care in getting riches; fear in keeping them, temptation in using them, guilt in abusing them; sorrow in losing them; and a burden of account at last to be given concerning them" (Ely, *I Quote*, 358).

II. FOCAL PASSAGES EXAMINED (1 Tim. 6:6-12,17-19)

In this lesson's focal verses, Paul wrote about money. First he offered advice to those who don't have it (vv. 6-8). Then he issued an alarm to those who want it (vv. 9-10). Finally he gave an admonition to those who have it (vv. 17-19).

1. Being Content (1 Tim. 6:6-8)

Someone said that money will not bring happiness, but it helps us to choose our misery. This may be true, but, as Paul told Timothy, true happiness comes through spiritual contentment. In verses 6-8 Paul first laid down a principle (v. 6); then he backed it up with two reasons (vv. 7-8).

Verses 6-8: **But godliness with contentment is great gain. For we brought nothing into this world, and it is certain we can carry nothing out. And having food and raiment let us be therewith content.**

In verse 5 Paul said people with worldly values often see prosperity as evidence of God's approval. They suppose "gain is godliness." By way of contrast, people with spiritual values turn that around. They know **godliness ... is great gain. Godliness** (*eusebeia*) refers to piety or religion. **Contentment** (*autarkeia*) was used by the Stoic philosophers of being self-sufficient or independent of external support. Paul used it of a mindset that is dependent on God alone. **Gain** (*porismos*) is used only in verses 5 and 6 in the New Testament. It refers to procuring, hence, **gain.** In verse 6 it does not refer to monetary wealth, as in verse 5, but to spiritual riches. True godliness with contentment is infinitely more valuable than a bulging bank account.

The first reason (indicated by the word **for**) we should be **content** is because we won't be staying here long and we can't take anything with us when we go. Verse 7 is a self-evident fact: **we brought nothing into this world, and it is certain we can carry nothing out.** It is also an allusion to the Old Testament (Job 1:21). The only thing that we go out of this world with that we did not bring into it is a shroud or burial cloth. And proverbial is the saying that there are no pockets in shrouds. When a rich man died, someone asked, "How much did he leave?" Another replied, "Every last cent." Alexander the Great gave instructions that when he died his hands were to be left outside his shroud. He wanted people to see that though he conquered the world, he left it empty-handed. To live all of life accumulating and hoarding money when we aren't staying here very long is foolish.

The second reason we should be **content** is that we have life's necessities. This reason is an allusion to Jesus' teaching (Matt. 6:25-34; Luke 12:22-31). Both words, **food** (*diatrophas*) and **raiment** (*skepasmata*; "clothing," NIV), are plural and are found only here in the New Testament. **Raiment** comes from the verb meaning "to cover" and could denote both clothing and shelter. However, Josephus (*Antiquities,* XV, 9.2) used it to mean food alone. Taken together, **food and raiment** are a figure of speech known as a *synecdoche,* in which a part is used for the whole, much as we would say "under my roof" to mean "in my house." In other words, **food and raiment** stand for "the necessities of life." So long as we have the necessities of life, we shall have all that we *need.* This does not mean we should not try to improve our position in life, but we should not do so at the expense of godliness.

Believers need to realize that godliness and contentment with life's basic necessities are keys toward developing a right attitude about money. Are you content with what you have?

2. Resisting Temptation (1 Tim. 6:9-10)

Several years ago I read of a survey conducted among university students. The only question asked concerned their reasons for getting an education. A large percentage answered, "To make money." This is the world's view of success. Paul warned against such an attitude.

Verse 9: **But they that will be rich fall into temptation and a snare, and into many foolish and hurtful lusts, which drown men in destruction and perdition.**

The Greek for **they that will be rich** reads "the ones willing [or wishing] to be rich." **But** is adversative, setting such over against those who were described as "content" in verses 6-8. The reference here concerns those whose one goal in life is to be rich, regardless of how they do it. Those with such an attitude pursue that goal, regardless of how many people they crush in doing it. To them the one great good is to be rich. Instead they **fall into temptation.** The **temptation** is to obtain wealth by dishonest means. The very chase after money is a **snare** or trap of Satan to bind people as his prey. **Lusts** means "desires." The desires may be good or bad, according to the context. Here the word is used in the evil sense, so the **lusts** are described as **foolish and hurtful.** In their pursuit of riches, they may hurt others, but they hurt themselves most of all–for these lusts **drown** them. This word means to pull down to the very bottom of **destruction and perdition. Perdition** renders *apoleian,* akin to Apollyon, which is one name for the devil (the destroyer).

The picture here is like the story of a man carrying a large sack of gold who came to a body of water. In trying to cross the water on a slippery log, he slipped and fell in. Had he turned loose of the bag of gold, he could have gotten out of the water with ease. But he held onto his gold, and the weight of it dragged him to the bottom where he drowned. Later, when his dead body was pulled from the water, he still was clutching his bag of gold to his chest.

Verse 10: **For the love of money is the root of all evil: which while some coveted after, they have erred from the faith, and pierced themselves through with many sorrows.**

We often hear people say, "Money is the root of all evil." Paul did not say that! He said, "The *love of money* is a root of every kind of evil (*panton,* 'all' without the definite article)." The

Greek text places the words **root of all evil** first in the sentence, making them emphatic. Also, in the Greek text, there is no definite article before **root.** There are other roots of evil, but **the love of money** (*philargyria*) is *a root* of much evil. Some people will commit any crime, even murder, for money. If handled properly, however, money may be the root of much good.

Coveted means "grabbed at" or "reached after." Those who grab at money err from **the faith,** that is, from the Christian faith. Such have been led away from, not to, the faith that centers in Jesus Christ. Too late, they find they have **pierced themselves through with many sorrows.** They have no one to blame but themselves. Their avarice has been the weapon with which they have committed spiritual suicide.

Money is a necessity and is not an evil in itself. But as Christians, we must keep money in proper perspective. Money cannot become the master we serve. As believers, we need to be aware that a consuming pursuit of money can endanger our faith and can cause us great grief. Resist the temptation!

3. Pursuing What Matters (1 Tim. 6:11-12)

Christians are to pursue with discipline those values and virtues that are in keeping with their calling and profession of faith in Christ.

Verse 11: **But thou, O man of God, flee these things; and follow after righteousness, godliness, faith, love, patience, meekness.**

But is adversative, setting Timothy over against the lovers of money. **Thou** (*su*) is emphatic since it opens the sentence. **Man of God** appears only twice in the New Testament. In 2 Timothy 3:17 the words are used in a general sense. While the expression is used here to refer to Timothy himself, that which follows may apply to anyone—man or woman—who serves the Lord.

Paul's admonition is both negative and positive. The two verbs, **flee** and **follow,** are present imperatives. They are commands to keep on doing these things. Negatively, we are to keep on fleeing from the love of money as if it were a plague or a vicious animal.

Positively, we are to keep on following or chasing after spiritual values. These are the true riches of life. **Righteousness** denotes living lives that are in keeping with the very nature of God. Akin to it is **godliness** or Godlikeness. Living by **faith** is to depend wholly on Christ, whose we are and whom we serve. **Love** (*agape*) does not ask, "What's in it for me?" Instead, it asks, "What can I contribute to meeting the needs of others?" The Greek word for **patience** was used in athletics and military life for the quality that enables one to take all his opponents could throw at him, yet still have reserve strength with which to countercharge to victory. It is "endurance" (NIV) in the face of trials. **Meekness** denotes the quality of being teachable. The word was used of trained, or tame, animals–animals that had been brought under control without breaking their spirits. Thus the word refers to power under control, or "gentleness" (NIV).

Verse 12: **Fight the good fight of faith, lay hold on eternal life, whereunto thou art also called, and hast professed a good profession before many witnesses.**

The related words that are both translated **fight** in the exhortation **fight the good fight of faith** are not adequate renderings of the Greek. Literally it reads, "*Agonize* (*agonizou*) the good *agony* (*agona*) of faith." Even this calls for explanation. The word for a Greek athletic contest was *agona*. The games consisted of many contests: races, boxing, wrestling, and so forth. The idea in such contests was to perform in order to be victorious. Paul, who was fond of using athletic terms in describing the Christian life, encouraged Christians to have a winning, conquering faith.

Lay hold on eternal life means to get a good grip on eternal life. This does not suggest the possibility of losing eternal life. Rather, we should live up to what we were **called** to be when we made our public **profession** of faith in Christ.

Having eternal life is more important than having temporal things. The antidote to materialism and the temptations inherent in having money is the pursuit of a Christlike character and lifestyle. Are you pursuing money or what really matters?

4. Making Money Serve (1 Tim. 6:17-19)

Verses 17-19 were written to people who already had money. Timothy was to teach **them that are rich in this world** the proper attitude toward and use of their money. This teaching was both negative and positive.

Verse 17: **Charge them that are rich in this world, that they be not high-minded, nor trust in uncertain riches, but in the living God, who giveth us richly all things to enjoy.**

Negatively, in verse 17, Paul said the rich were not to be **high-minded,** nor **trust in uncertain riches.** The Greek text begins with "to the rich in the now age [*nun aioni*]." Being placed at the beginning of the sentence, this phrase is emphatic. Timothy, first, was to **charge** the presently rich not to be **high-minded** or "arrogant" (NIV). That is, they were not to be inordinately proud of their riches–stuck up. Second, they were not to place their **trust** or "hope" (NIV) in the uncertainty of riches. Riches have a way of sprouting wings and flying away. One unfavorable word out of Washington or a change in international conditions can send the stock market into a tailspin! Instead, they were to trust **in the living God,** who gives **all things** that afford lasting joy. God is stable, in contrast to the instability of worldly riches.

Verses 18-19: **That they do good, that they be rich in good works, ready to distribute, willing to communicate; laying up in store for themselves a good foundation against the time to come, that they may lay hold on eternal life.**

Positively, in verses 18-19, Paul gave four ways the rich were to use their money wisely. First, they were to **do good** (*agatho-ergein;* from *agathos,* "good," and *ergo,* "work"; used only here and in Acts 14:17 in the New Testament). That is, they were to use their money in positive ways. Second, they were to **be rich in good works** (*en ergois kalois,* a different word for **good**). It is more important to be rich in good works than to be rich in monetary wealth. The more money one has, the greater potential one has for doing good—and the greater obligation. Third, they were to be **ready to distribute** their wealth. **Ready to distribute** renders a compound adjective (*eumetadotos*; from *eu*, "good" or "noble," and *metadidomi*, "give a share of") that is used only here in the New Testament. It means "to be liberal in giving to others in need" or "be generous" (NIV). Fourth, they were to be **willing to communicate** (*koinonikous*) or "willing to share" (NIV). This adjective, also used only here in the New Testament, is akin to the word for fellowship or sharing, *koinonia*—having all things in common. Christians should regard money as a trust from God to be shared with others, not as something to be hoarded for their own selfish indulgence.

By being generous, Paul wrote, the rich were doing two things. First, they were **laying up in store for themselves a good foundation against the time to come. Laying up in store** (*apothesaurizontas*) is a compound and intensive verb used only here in the New Testament. It means "to lay up treasures." Paul's teaching here echoed Jesus' teaching in Matthew 6:19-21. Notice the words **for themselves.** In giving to others, we may think we are helping only them, but actually we bless ourselves. **The time to come** (*to mellon*) means "the things about to happen." The word can refer to any future time, either now or eternity. In fact, both are included here.

Second, they were really living. The best texts do not read **that they may lay hold on eternal life** but "so that they may take hold of the life that is truly life" (NIV) or "life indeed" (*tes ontos zoes*). People who selfishly hoard their wealth are merely existing. "Life indeed" is sharing. Sharing enriches your life here and now, and it amasses spiritual treasures in heaven. Paradoxical though it may seem, we gain by sharing; we keep by giving. By using our possessions to help others, by cultivating generosity and sharing what we have, we show that our priorities are spiritual. So make your money your servant, not your master.

August 17

PREJUDICE

Basic Passage: Acts 10:1–11:18
Focal Passages: Acts 10:9-16,27-29a,34-35; 11:15-18

INTRODUCTION

1. *Prejudice* means what the word says. It is the attitude of *pre-judging* others, or judging beforehand. The dictionary defines it as a hasty, premature judgment; a bias, favorable or unfavorable: usually an unreasoning objection to a person or thing; injury or harm as the result of hasty or unfair judgment. Prejudice is expressed in the saying, "Don't confuse me with facts; my mind is already made up."

2. Some people try to justify their ethnic prejudices from the Bible. But a proper understanding of the Bible does not support such, as will be seen by examining this lesson's focal verses.

3. The Central Bible Truth of this lesson is that God shows no prejudice toward anyone and expects His people to overcome prejudice in their lives.

4. The purpose of this lesson is to help you understand why prejudice is a sin and commit yourself to overcoming it.

5. This lesson seeks to answer the question, Why should I overcome my prejudices?

I. SOME PRELIMINARY CONSIDERATIONS

1. The Background

After being engaged in an itinerant ministry in the western part of Palestine (Acts 9:32), Peter visited Lydda, where he healed a paralytic named Aeneas [ih-NEE-uhs]. When news of the healing spread to Joppa (modern Jaffa), the ancient seaport

for Jerusalem on the Mediterranean coast, the believers there
sent for Peter because a disciple named Tabitha (Hebrew) or Dor-
cas (Greek) had died. Peter restored her to life and remained in
Joppa for some time (9:43). Then, as a result of two visions from
God—one to Cornelius (10:1-8) and one to Peter (10:9-16)—Peter
went to Caesarea [sehs-uh-REE-uh], the seaport 30 miles to the
north, where he preached in the home of the Roman soldier Cornelius. When Peter returned to Jerusalem, he was confronted by
those "that were of the circumcision" about his actions.

2. Essentials for Overcoming Prejudice

To understand the problem of prejudice is the first step toward
its solution. For this to be done, at least three things are essential: (a) to recognize a problem exists; (b) to examine its cause;
and (c) to seek its cure with an open mind and heart. May these
things be uppermost in the minds of all who study this lesson.

II. FOCAL PASSAGES EXAMINED
(Acts 10:9-16,27-29a,34-35; 11:15-18)

Peter was a Jew. He had serious prejudices toward Gentiles.
He especially had a problem with respect to the relationship between Jews and Gentiles in the church. When *confronted* with
his prejudice, Peter *resisted* change. It took a vision from God and
a demonstration by the Holy Spirit for Peter to begin to change.
After he was forced to confront his prejudices and to begin to deal
with them, Peter defended the mission to the Gentiles at the
Jerusalem Conference (Acts 15:7-11). However, sometime later, in
Antioch, Peter regressed considerably over the Jew-Gentile question (Gal. 2:11-14). Ultimately, Peter *overcame* his prejudices.
That Peter won the victory over his prejudices and sought to *influence* others about the dangers of prejudice is seen in 1 Peter
2:1-10 where he declared that Christians are the true people of
God regardless of race, nationality, class, or any other factor.

1. Confronting Prejudice (Acts 10:9-13)

Cornelius was a military centurion–a commander of 100 Roman soldiers–in "the Italian Regiment" (10:1; NIV), a portion of which was stationed in Caesarea. Caesarea was the resident city of the Roman procurator (governor) of Judea, Samaria, and Idumea [id-yoo-MEE-uh]. Cornelius is described as devout, God-fearing, generous with alms to a captive people, and a man of prayer (v. 2). While Cornelius was praying at 3 p.m., "the ninth hour of the day" (v. 3)–one of the three daily prayer times for Jews–he had a vision in which he saw an angel telling him to send to Joppa for Simon Peter (vv. 5-6). Cornelius then sent two household servants to Joppa. He also sent a devout soldier with them for their protection (v. 7). Apparently the messengers left immediately, spending the night along the way (v. 8).

10:9-10: **On the morrow, as they went on their journey, and drew nigh unto the city, Peter went up upon the housetop to pray about the sixth hour: and he became very hungry, and would have eaten: but while they made ready, he fell into a trance.**

The next day, as Cornelius's messengers neared Joppa, **Peter went up upon the housetop to pray.** Houses in Palestine had flat roofs. It was the **sixth hour** according to the Jewish reckoning of time, or "noon" (NIV), another Jewish prayer time.

The sixth hour was not only prayer time; it also was meal time. Peter **became very hungry** (*prospeinos*), a rare word used only here in the New Testament, **and would have eaten.** The text literally says, he "desired to eat." The verb is an imperfect tense. Peter apparently could smell the food being **made ready,** and the aroma caused him to begin to desire food and continue to do so. At that time and in that condition, Peter **fell into a trance.** Literally, "an ecstasy (*ekstasis*) came upon him." "Ecstasy" means to be in a state in which consciousness is wholly or partially suspended and one feels as if he or she is standing outside of oneself (see 22:17).

10:11-13: **And saw heaven opened, and a certain vessel descending unto him, as it had been a great sheet knit at the four corners, and let down to the earth: wherein were all manner of fourfooted beasts of the earth, and wild beasts, and creeping things, and fowls of the air. And there came a voice to him, Rise, Peter; kill, and eat.**

In his ecstatic state or vision Peter saw something like a large sheet lowered out of heaven **to the earth.** In it was every variety of animals, both clean and unclean **(fourfooted beasts . . . and wild beasts),** snakes **(creeping things),** and birds **(fowls of the air).**

According to the Mosaic law, certain kinds of flesh were unclean and were not to be eaten by the Israelites (see Lev. 11). Even certain fish were forbidden as food (see Deut. 14:9). However, in Mark 7:15-23 Jesus taught that it was not what went into people but what came out of them that defiled them. Thus, "Jesus declared all foods 'clean'" (v. 19; NIV).

But the problem was not one of dietary restrictions; it was one of ethnic prejudice. The Jews had transferred the concepts of *clean* and *unclean* to people. Jews were clean; non-Jews were unclean. This had become a part of the "wall" separating Jews from Gentiles (Eph. 2:14). Prejudice lay at the heart of the problem of getting Jewish Christians to preach the gospel to non-Jews. God was preparing Peter to go witness to Cornelius. This vision was an expression of God's love for all people. It was designed to confront Peter with his prejudice and help him overcome it.

Peter heard **a voice** telling him to **kill** and **eat** without discrimination. Peter recognized the **voice** as God's voice, since he called him **Lord.** But, true to Peter's nature, he argued with God.

2. Resisting Change (Acts 10:14-16)

None of us like to be confronted with the need to change our deep-seated options and prejudices. We resist making needed changes. So did Peter.

10:14-16: **But Peter said, Not so, Lord; for I have never eaten anything that is common or unclean. And the voice spake unto him again the second time, What God hath cleansed, that call not thou common. This was done thrice: and the vessel was received up again into heaven.**

Not so translates *medamos.* A. T. Robertson (*Word Pictures in the New Testament,* vol. 3 [Nashville: Broadman Press, 1930], 136) noted Peter did not use *oudamos,* "a blunt refusal (I shall not do it)." He then added, "And yet it is more than a mild protest. . . . It is a polite refusal with a reason given." Literally, Peter said, "Because at no time did I eat any single thing common or unclean." As hungry as he was, Peter would not break the Jewish dietary laws. Then the voice came again and said **what God hath cleansed** he was not to call **common.** The Greek uses **thou** (*su*) emphatically, "You not make common"–setting Peter over against God. A third time this happened, but still Peter did not obey. Then the sheet was taken back to heaven.

The vision left Peter perplexed: "Peter doubted in himself what this vision which he had seen should mean" (v. 17). "In himself" is in the emphatic position, preceding the verb. "Doubted" renders a verb that means "to be completely at a loss to know what road to take" (Robertson, *Word Pictures,* vol. 3, 138). The imperfect tense shows Peter began and continued to be in this state of mind.

Peter was a religious man–but a prejudiced one. How like him are multitudes of Christians in their deep-seated prejudices! Strange bedfellows, but religion and prejudice often are found in the same heart. Racial prejudice is bad enough in ungodly people; it is worse in Christian people. God was showing Peter that He made no distinction between Jews and Gentiles. Peter, however, missed the point. He was resisting God. He forgot everything Jesus taught him about this! God is not prejudiced. No person is despised by God because of race or ethnic background. So no one should despise another person in regard to race–or any other outward differences. *In God's sight, the prejudiced person is more unclean than the one who is the object of prejudice.*

But we know that when people are confronted with their prejudices, they resist change. As believers we need to recognize our resistance to overcoming our prejudices. We need to be willing to change our attitudes toward other people. In Christ God had met Peter's spiritual hungers—and He proposed to do the same for Cornelius, having chosen Peter as His human instrument to do so. Similarly, in Christ God has met our spiritual hunger. As Jesus' followers, we must not permit outward differences or inward prejudices to prevent us from doing our Christian duty.

3. Overcoming Prejudice (Acts 10:27-29a,34-35)

While Peter pondered the meaning of this vision, the men sent by Cornelius arrived. Peter went down to the messengers and asked why they sought him. The men related Cornelius's experience (v. 22), and Peter invited them to spend the night. The next morning they all set out for Caesarea, accompanied by "certain brethren," or Jewish Christians, from Joppa (v. 23).

Cornelius was so certain Peter would come that he had gathered together "his kinsmen" (probably his family) and some close friends. When Cornelius saw Peter coming, he ran and "fell down at his feet, and worshiped him" (v. 25). Since Cornelius was a God-fearer who worshiped the one true God, we hardly can see him worshiping another man. Cornelius's action probably was an expression of his humility, appreciation, and sense of unworthiness. Peter, however, either mistook Cornelius's action as worship or he was afraid others would interpret it as such. So Peter said, "Stand up; I myself also am a man" (v. 26).

10:27-29a: And as he talked with him, he went in, and found many that were come together. And he said unto them, Ye know how that it is an unlawful thing for a man that is a Jew to keep company, or come unto one of another nation; but God hath showed me that I should not call any man common or unclean. Therefore came I unto you without gainsaying, as soon as I was sent for.

Peter went inside and saw the other Gentiles gathered in Cornelius's house. Peter said to the Gentiles, **Ye know how that it is an unlawful thing for a man that is a Jew to keep company, or come unto one of another nation.** What a way to begin a friendly conversation! Yet the emphatic use of **ye** shows this was a well-known fact. We would say "You yourselves" (NASB, NRSV). **One of another nation** (*allophulo*) literally is "one of another race." The Greek word is used only here in the New Testament, but from the Jewish perspective it meant "a foreigner," "a pagan," or "a Gentile" (NIV). **Unlawful** translates a Greek word that also may be translated "not according to custom." Since the Mosaic law does not forbid social contact between Israelites and Gentiles, Peter was not describing a violation of that law. He had reference to what the rabbis taught and to what had become a social custom among Jews (for example, see the Jewish Mishnah, *Demai* 2.3.4). Long practice, as in the American South, had made their prejudice a matter of common law.

Then Peter added, **but God hath showed me that I should not call any man common or unclean.** In the Greek text this portion of the verse begins with *kamoi,* a combination of *kai* (meaning "and" or "but") and *moi* ("to me"). In this context *kai* has the sense of "but," an adversative that sets God over against custom—"but to me." Despite what custom said, God told Peter **not to call any man common or unclean.** Notice Peter used the word for "no one" (*medena*), not the word for "no thing." Apparently Peter still would obey Jewish dietary laws taught in the Mosaic code, but he would not follow the current custom of applying the laws of clean and unclean to people.

Since God had instructed Peter to go to Cornelius's house, Peter said he went **without gainsaying,** or without raising any questions, and **as soon as I was sent for.** Now that he was there, Peter asked why the Roman centurion had sent for him (v. 29). Cornelius told Peter about his experience with the Lord (vv. 30-33). When Peter heard about the officer's vision, he then understood his own vision. So Peter proceeded to preach the gospel to Cornelius and those with him.

10:34-35: Then Peter opened his mouth, and said, Of a truth I perceive that God is no respecter of persons: but in every nation he that feareth him, and worketh righteousness, is accepted with him.

Of a truth may read "truly" (NRSV). **Perceive** translates a verb that means "to take hold down" or "really to take hold of" something. Robertson (*Word Pictures,* vol. 3, 143) said the middle (reflexive) voice, as here, denotes mental action, to lay hold with the mind. In colloquial language we would say, "I've really got it!"

What was this great idea Peter now had in his firm grasp? **That God is no respecter of persons. Respecter of persons** is a compound word composed of three parts: *pros,* before; *ops,* eye or face; and *lambano,* to take hold. The resultant word is *prosopolemptes.* The first two words combined make *prosopon,* face. Robertson (*Word Pictures,* vol. 3, 143) said, "The idea is to pay regard to one's looks [face] or circumstances rather than to his intrinsic character." **No** renders the strong negative *ouk.* God does not judge a person by his or her face—or racial characteristics. God shows no prejudice. The Jews thought they were God's favorites to the exclusion of all others. Peter said he now saw that was not true. Instead, **in every nation** or ethnic group (*ethnei*) those who reverence God **(feareth him)** and work **righteousness** are **accepted** by Him. These words do not indicate that people can earn salvation. Rather, they suggest God looks into people's hearts. He judges by their hearts, not by their faces.

Peter accepted Cornelius upon God's appraisal. Even as he preached to him and his household, the Holy Spirit came upon them as evidence that they had believed in Jesus as Savior (v. 44; see John 14:16 and Eph. 1:13a-14). At Peter's word, these new Christians were baptized (vv. 46-48).

Believers are to follow God's example in relating to other people. God shows no prejudice but is open to all people. Christians are to accept all those whom God accepts, without prejudice.

4. Influencing Others (Acts 11:15-18)

Word of this event reached Jerusalem before Peter arrived. As soon as he returned, Peter was called on the carpet by his fellow apostles and other Christians in Jerusalem about going into a Gentile's home and eating with Gentiles (11:1-3). However, after hearing Peter's account of the entire event, they could not deny this was a genuine work of God's grace (vv. 4-18).

Verses 15-17 are the climax of Peter's defense against Jewish prejudice. Peter presented evidence that could not be denied.

11:15-17: **And as I began to speak, the Holy Ghost** [Spirit] **fell on them, as on us at the beginning. Then remembered I the word of the Lord, how that he said, John indeed baptized with water; but ye shall be baptized with the Holy Ghost** [Spirit]. **Forasmuch then as God gave them the like gift as he did unto us, who believed on the Lord Jesus Christ; what was I, that I could withstand God?**

Peter did not repeat the content of his sermon on this occasion. He simply said that as he preached to Cornelius, the Holy Spirit came upon Cornelius and his household the moment they believed in Jesus **as on us at the beginning** (see John 14:17 and Acts 2). Peter's six companions could verify the fact (v. 12). This experience reminded Peter of the promise Jesus made just prior to His ascension (Acts 1:5).

All along Peter had stressed that this was a work of God. Now he drew his conclusion: **God gave them the like gift as he did unto us . . . what was I, that I could withstand God?** It certainly was not Peter's idea to go to a Gentile's house and share the good news. He knew he was running into the face of Jewish racial prejudice. Nevertheless, when it came to holding on to his prejudice or doing God's will, Peter had no choice: "Who was I to think that I could oppose God?" (NIV). He had to obey God. Like Peter, believers today are to stand against prejudice even when we are criticized or opposed for our stance.

11:18: **When they heard these things, they held their peace, and glorified God, saying, Then hath God also to the Gentiles granted repentance unto life.**

Peter's final words "silenced" (NRSV) his critics. Even the Judaizers could not question that this was a work of God. The group could only praise God. In the Greek text, **to the Gentiles** is emphatic: "To the Gentiles of all people" God granted repentance unto "salvation life" (*zoen*).

Granted (*edoken*) is an aorist tense, but it is translated in most versions as if it were a perfect tense—**hath . . . granted.** The perfect tense expresses action in the past that is still true in the present, with the implication that it will continue to be true in the future. On the other hand, the aorist tense simply states that a thing happened. Thus, while the Jerusalem church accepted the case of Cornelius and his household and friends, perhaps they regarded this as an isolated instance instead of a permanent and general fact (T. C. Smith, "Acts," *The Broadman Bible Commentary,* vol. 10 [Nashville: Broadman Press, 1970], 71; Frank Stagg, *The Book of Acts,* [Nashville: Broadman Press, 1955], 123). Subsequent events show that the more conservative element in the Jerusalem church tended to have difficulty overcoming their deep-seated prejudices (see Acts 15) and, despite all of Paul's future efforts, the Jerusalem church never committed itself to Gentile missions.

All around the world there are many excuses people give for being prejudiced. Factors such as race, caste, economic status, tribal heritage, cultural background, and religious beliefs are at the core of much of the world's bloodshed. When we as believers overcome prejudices, we often influence other people to confront their prejudices and to take steps toward removing them. But prejudice dies a hard, slow death. And as believers we too must keep working at it. In the final analysis it comes down to you. Do you need to change? Are you willing to change now? By God's grace we too will win the victory.

August 24

VIOLENCE

Basic Passages: Genesis 6:5-13; Psalm 55:4-11;
Jonah 3:3-10; 1 Peter 3:9-12
Focal Passages: Genesis 6:11-13; Psalm 55:9-11;
Jonah 3:6-10; 1 Peter 3:9-12

INTRODUCTION

1. There is no denying that we live in a violent world. Even those who have not been victims of a violent crime themselves know this is true. All one has to do is to watch the nightly news broadcasts to confirm this fact.

2. This lesson seeks to answer the question, What can I do about the violence in my society?

3. The Central Bible Truth of this lesson is that God condemns violence; thus, believers are to call for people to turn from violence and are to counter evil with good.

4. The purpose of this lesson is to help you decide one way you will oppose violence in your society.

I. SOME PRELIMINARY CONSIDERATIONS

1. The Background

Genesis 6 describes the condition of the world prior to the great flood and announces God's judgment on the corrupt and violent world. Psalm 55 is a psalm of David. Its superscription, "To the chief Musician on Neginoth," indicates the song was designed to be accompanied "with stringed instruments" (NIV). In this psalm David lamented the violence of his city and expressed his fear of violence. Jonah 3 tells the story of the response of the people of Nineveh, the capital city of the Assyrian Empire, to

Jonah's preaching–possibly in the time of Assur-dan III (771-754 B.C.). The Ninevites rejected violence and their evil ways, and the city was spared. In all likelihood, Peter wrote his first letter about A.D. 62-64 during the persecution under Nero. He addressed it to "the exiles of the Dispersion" (1:1, NRSV). "Dispersion" renders *diasporas,* which comes from the word meaning "to scatter seed." *Diaspora* long had been used of Jews living outside Palestine. Peter used the term to refer to Christians, probably both Jews and Gentiles, who lived in the Roman provinces mentioned in 1:1. He told his readers how they should respond to violence as Christians.

2. Violence in Society

We live in a violent age. We watch violence on TV, read about it in the newspapers, hear it booming from radios, and see it with our eyes. From childhood we are bombarded by violent scenes. Violence takes many forms–including physical harm, all sorts of abuses, and verbal comments. Violence uses many weapons. Many countries are torn apart by those who have accepted revolutionary violence as a means of bringing about social change. Through their acts, violent people often are idolized and turned into heroes. Violence occurs in society, in the workplace, and even in homes. No *place* is immune from it. It occurs in all ages of people and at all levels of income. No *person* is immune from it.

II. FOCAL PASSAGES EXAMINED
   (Gen. 6:11-13; Ps. 55:9-11; Jonah 3:6-10; 1 Pet. 3:9-12)

Both the Old and the New Testaments condemn the use of violence. Violence invites God's judgment and destroys the infrastructure of society and culture. God is compassionate to those who reject violence. He expects His people to pursue peace and to be a blessing to others.

1. Judgment on Violence (Gen. 6:11-13)

Violence has marked every society from humanity's early history until now. Because of this fact, some people accept violence as a natural societal occurrence and even justify its existence. Believers, however, are to recognize that a society marked by violence is not God's desire and is in danger of God's judgment.

Verses 11-13: **The earth also was corrupt before God, and the earth was filled with violence. And God looked upon the earth, and, behold, it was corrupt; for all flesh had corrupted his way upon the earth. And God said unto Noah, The end of all flesh is come before me; for the earth is filled with violence through them; and, behold, I will destroy them with the earth.**

Earth does not refer merely to land area but includes the people living on the earth. Two things are said about the earth: it **was corrupt before God,** and it **was filled with violence.** It is tragic to compare this description with Genesis 1:31. There the created order, along with the human occupants, was declared "very good." Here the earth, with its human occupants, was declared *very bad.* **Flesh** refers to human beings. Evil people corrupt whatever they touch.

The word **destroy** means "to blot out" or "erase." Universal sin called for universal judgment—not because God is sadistic and enjoys punishing people, but because God is righteous and holy and cannot ignore sin. Total depravity called for total destruction of the unrepentant depraved.

2. Fear of Violence (Ps. 55:9-11)

Good citizens always are distressed by the violence in their cities. But as king, David was challenged directly by it. He was fearful of the widespread and constant violence that was tearing Jerusalem apart and destroying it from within. So he took the problem to God in prayer, calling on the Lord to intervene.

Verses 9-11: **Destroy, O Lord, and divide their tongues: for I have seen violence and strife in the city. Day and night they go about it upon the walls thereof: mischief also and sorrow are in the midst of it. Wickedness is in the midst thereof: deceit and guile depart not from her streets.**

These verses are in the form of a complaint addressed to the **Lord** (*Adonai*), the Master of the world. David personified the evil characteristics that had taken over the city, naming seven of them. The first two, **violence** and **strife,** he described as watchmen on the city's **walls.** The city was "protected" by deadly watchmen. The chief residents who dwelt **in the midst** of the city were **mischief** ("malice," NIV), **sorrow** ("abuse," NIV), and **wickedness** ("destructive forces," NIV). David said that the last two, **deceit and guile** or "threats and lies" (NIV), never left "the public square." The Hebrew word rendered **streets** referred to "the broad open space in a town, usually near the gate, where social, business, and legal affairs were conducted" (Tate, "Psalms 51–100," 57). Thus violence ruled wherever–**upon the walls** or in the **streets**–and whenever–**day and night**–he looked.

David asked the Lord to repeat two actions to these violent people that He had done earlier in Israel's history. First, David asked the Lord to **destroy** them. **Destroy** literally means "swallow up"–not "confound," "frustrate," or "confuse" (NIV) them. David called on the Lord to swallow them up or remove them as He did with Korah and his fellow rebels when they rebelled against Moses and Aaron (Num. 16:29-33). Since the violent bring harm on others, David asked the Lord to bring harm on them. Second, David asked the Lord to **divide their tongues. Divide their tongues** literally is "split their tongue." This apparently is a reference to the incident at the tower of Babel when the Lord confounded the languages of the people (Gen. 11:5-9). The destructive forces had done so much damage with their tongues, David prayed that the evil instigated by their tongues might turn upon themselves, devouring them rather than destroying the city.

When a society is overwhelmed by violence and its people are gripped by the fear of violence, believers are to turn to the Lord and ask for His help.

3. Rejection of Violence (Jonah 3:6-10)

After reluctantly going to Nineveh, the capital of the ruthless Assyrian Empire, Jonah proclaimed the Lord's message, warning the people of coming disaster and calling on them to repent.

Verses 6-9: **For word came unto the king of Nineveh, and he arose from his throne, and he laid his robe from him, and covered him with sackcloth, and sat in ashes. And he caused it to be proclaimed and published through Nineveh by the decree of the king and his nobles, saying, Let neither man nor beast, herd nor flock, taste anything: let them not feed, nor drink water: but let man and beast be covered with sackcloth, and cry mightily unto God: yea, let them turn everyone from his evil way, and from the violence that is in their hands. Who can tell if God will turn and repent, and turn away from his fierce anger, that we perish not?**

Jonah preached in the streets, not in the palace. However, news of his preaching and the wave of repentance that swept through the city reached the palace. Instead of ordering Jonah's arrest, **the king** responded favorably to his message. He **arose from his throne,** took off his embroidered royal **robe** and kingly trappings, donned **sackcloth, and sat in ashes. Sackcloth** was a coarse fabric made from goat's hair. To put on sackcloth and sit on ashes was a sign of mourning for the dead, grieving over one's sins, or deep humiliation (1 Kings 20:31; Isa. 15:3; Jer. 49:3; Ezek. 27:31).

Crisis times call for strong measures. The king summoned all **his nobles,** and they issued a decree that called for four responses to Jonah's preaching: universal fasting, wearing sackcloth, pleading with God, and turning from evil and violence. First, both people (*'adam,* **man** in the generic sense) and their animals **(beast, herd, flock)** were to refrain from food and

water. Total fasting denoted total repentance. Second, the people were to put **sackcloth** on their animals. This showed the people's degree of repentance. Third, the people were to **cry mightily unto God.** This would be the God of Jonah, since it was He who threatened to destroy the city. Fourth, the king's decree brought the guilt down to the individual person. As further proof of their repentance, **everyone** (*'ish,* every individual person) of them was to **turn from his evil way** and **from the violence that is in their hands. Evil way** includes all wickedness condemned by the law. **Violence** (*hamas*) refers to specific physical acts of wrong, wild, ruthless living. It is defiance of the law by one who is too strong to be brought to account. **Turn** (*shub*) is the Hebrew word for repentance, which involves an "about face" or complete change in one's life.

The king concluded his edict by stating, **Who can tell,** or "Who knows?" (NIV), **if God will turn and repent, and turn away from his fierce anger, that we perish not?** Jonah made no specific promise to this effect. This was not a stated fact but an expressed hope. **Fierce anger** (*meharon 'appo*) literally reads "the burning of his nose," referring to breathing or snorting and the flushed color produced by anger. **That we perish not** denotes being rescued from the grip of death. It may read, "that we might not keep on dying."

The words **turn and repent** that are applied to God in verse 9 call for special attention. **Turn** (*shub*) is the same word that was used for human repentance from sin in verse 8. But since God has no imperfections, the meaning cannot be the same as in verse 8. **Repent** translates the Hebrew verb *niham*—which expresses deep sorrow for and participation in the grief of another, resulting in action that brings comfort to the other. To soften the idea that God turns and repents, the *New International Version* renders the first word "relent" and the second word "with compassion turn." The meaning is that the king hoped God might *turn back* the impending disaster and destruction He had pronounced on Nineveh through Jonah—which was God's intention all along (see 4:2).

Verse 10: **And God saw their works, that they turned from their evil way; and God repented of the evil, that he had said that he would do unto them; and he did it not.**

True repentance expresses itself in a changed lifestyle. The genuineness of the Ninevites' repentance was seen in their **works** or "deeds." Nineveh **turned** or "repented" (*shub*) from their **evil way** (*ra'a*), and God **repented** (the same word as in v. 9) of **the evil** (*ra'a*) He planned to do. The *New International Version,* again wishing to avoid the idea of God repenting, states that God "had compassion." **Evil** (*ra'a*), when used of the Ninevites, means moral evil; but when the word is used of God, it should be translated "trouble," "calamity," or "destruction" (NIV) since God does not do moral evil. When Nineveh repented, the Lord expressed His deep sorrow over the terrible punishment He had planned. What the king had hoped for (v. 9) actually happened (v. 10).

Like Jonah, Christians can proclaim the hope that when a society rejects and turns from its evil and violent ways, God will have compassion and will withhold His judgment upon it.

4. Response to Violence (1 Pet. 3:9-12)

In the midst of a violent society, believers are to reject retaliation and pursue peace. We are to counter evil actions and verbal abuse with blessing.

Verses 9-12: **Not rendering evil for evil, or railing for railing: but contrariwise blessing; knowing that ye are thereunto called, that ye should inherit a blessing. For he that will love life, and see good days, let him refrain his tongue from evil, and his lips that they speak no guile: let him eschew evil, and do good; let him seek peace, and ensue it. For the eyes of the Lord are over the righteous, and his ears are open unto their prayers: but the face of the Lord is against them that do evil.**

When Christians respond to evil, we should not return **evil for evil** (see Rom. 12:17 for Paul's identical statement) or **railing for railing** ("insult with insult," NIV). Instead, we should respond with acts of **blessing.** To *bless* (*eulogein*; from *eu,* good, and *logos,* word) means "to speak well of" someone. But here it has a distinctly religious sense—"to extend to someone the prospect of salvation, or the favor of God." This is what believers **are . . . called** to do since we will **inherit a blessing** (salvation) from the Lord.

It takes two to make a fight. More moral courage is needed not to retaliate than to return evil for evil. If you return evil for evil, you descend to the level of the one who did evil to you. Peter counseled returning blessing for evil done to us. Proverbial is the saying, "To return evil for good is animal-like; to return evil for evil is human-like; to return good for evil is God-like."

To emphasize his point, Peter quoted freely Psalm 34:12-16 in verses 10-12. **He that will** is *ho thelon,* "the one willing, wishing, or desiring." **Love** renders *agapan.* **Life** translates *zoen,* the spiritual quality of life—or salvation life—not merely biological life (*bios*). If one wills to have such life and to **see good days,** Peter stressed in verses 10b-11 that he should do five things (all are third person singular imperatives ending in -*ato*): first, **let him refrain** or guard or "keep" (NIV) **his tongue from evil, and his lips that they speak no guile** or "deceitful speech" (NIV); second, **let him eschew** or avoid or "turn from" (NIV) **evil**; third, let him **do good**; fourth, **let him seek peace**; fifth, let him **ensue** or "pursue" (NIV) **it** (peace). Then Peter concluded by focusing on the **eyes, ears,** and **face** of the Lord. On the one hand, **the eyes of the Lord are** watching **over the righteous, and his ears are open** to hear **their prayers.** On the other hand, **the face** or countenance **of the Lord is against them that do evil.**

What can you do about violence in your society? Some Christians are in positions of authority to do something about violence and violent offenders. Most Christians are not in such positions. But all Christians can respond personally to violence as Christ would have us to; and we can minister to victims of violence by providing comfort, protection, shelter, food, clothing, counseling, legal assistance, and other forms of help as needed. How will you be a *blessing*? What *good* will you do?

ALCOHOL AND DRUGS

Basic Passages: Proverbs 20:1; 23:19-21,29-35
Focal Passages: Proverbs 20:1; 23:19-21,29-35

INTRODUCTION

1. This lesson deals with one of the greatest and most rapidly growing problems in our society today–the use of alcohol and illegal drugs. This issue affects all economic and social levels of our society–and even has become a problem among Christians.

2. What the Bible says about alcohol equally is true of other illegal narcotics as well.

3. The Central Bible Truth of this lesson is that adults demonstrate wisdom in abstaining from alcohol and illegal drugs because of the dangers involved.

4. The purpose of this lesson is to help you decide to avoid the present and future dangers of alcohol and illegal drugs by abstaining from these substances.

5. This lesson seeks to answer the question, Why should I abstain from drinking alcoholic beverages or using illegal drugs?

I. SOME PRELIMINARY CONSIDERATIONS

1. The Background

The Book of Proverbs is composed of eight collections of wise sayings, five of which have brief superscriptions or introductions identifying the author or compiler. Proverbs 20:1 is a proverb of Solomon that is contained in a collection of his proverbs that runs from 10:1–22:16. Proverbs 23 is from a group of anonymous wise sayings that runs from 22:17–24:22.

2. The Main Reason to Avoid Alcohol and Drugs

There are valid physical, economic, social, and health reasons that make it wise for all human beings to abstain from drinking alcohol and taking illegal drugs. Believers, however, also have a religious reason why we should avoid abusing these substances and the activities often associated with their abuse—God, in His Word, has said to do so (Luke 21:34; Rom. 13:13; Eph. 5:18; 1 Thess. 5:7-8; 1 Pet. 4:3). Thus believers are to avoid abusing alcohol and drugs as part of our Christian commitment, not merely because of the natural adverse effects such substances have on our bodies or because of other unfavorable social consequences.

II. FOCAL PASSAGES EXAMINED
   (Prov. 20:1; 23:19-21,29-35)

These focal verses in Proverbs 20 and 23 warn against and describe the effects of alcohol and other narcotics.

1. The Corrupting Power of Alcohol (Prov. 20:1)

Verse 1: **Wine is a mocker, strong drink is raging: and whoever is deceived thereby is not wise.**

Wine and **strong drink,** "beer" (NIV), refer to alcoholic beverages. Alcoholic beverages mock everything that is high and holy. Alcohol especially mocks those who imbibe it. Alcohol seems to promise much, but it pays off in misery to those who are enslaved to it. It is **a mocker** indeed.

Marvin E. Tate, Jr. ("Proverbs," in *The Broadman Bible Commentary,* vol. 5 [Nashville: Broadman Press, 1971], 63) pointed out that the "normal use of wine on festal occasions was accepted" in the Bible (see Prov. 3:10; 9:2,5; Eccl. 9:7; Ps. 104:15; Job 1:13). However, in our social climate it is best for Christians to avoid such. Further, even in that ancient climate the prophets condemned the excessive use of intoxicating beverages (see Amos 6:6; Hos. 7:5; Isa. 5:11-12,22; Jer. 23:9).

Raging may read "brawler" (NIV), stressing the result of intoxication. **Deceived** translates a Hebrew word that has the basic meaning "to be led astray" or "to err." In the context of alcohol, however, it is a term for intoxication and means "to stagger drunkenly"–"to swerve," "to meander," "to reel," or "to roll" in drunkenness (see Isa. 28:7). Further, the one who indulges in alcoholic beverages **is not wise,** that is, "does not act wisely." The words also may be translated "cannot act wisely."

Alcohol has powerful effects on the lives of those who use it. It can make them scoffers, involve them in physical violence, and rob them of mental and physical coordination. We are wise to avoid any practice that deprives us of self-control.

2. Wise Action Regarding Alcohol (Prov. 23:19-20)

Those who act wisely do not participate in the activities of those who abuse alcohol–or, for that matter, in activities that involve any illegal drug.

Verses 19-20: **Hear thou, my son, and be wise, and guide thine heart in the way. Be not among winebibbers; among riotous eaters of flesh.**

Hear thou, my son indicates the format of a father or other wise counselor speaking to a young man. This style is found throughout the Book of Proverbs.

The **son** or pupil is admonished to be **wise** by learning the instruction of his teacher and by keeping his **heart** or mind **in the way** of wisdom. The idea in **guide** or "direct" (NRSV) is to be straight. The point is for him to get his mind straight about his way of life. The *New International Version* has "keep your heart on the right path."

Specifically, the counselor warned against being among **winebibbers** or "drunkards" (NIV) and **riotous eaters of flesh** or "gluttons" (NIV). The figure is that of the debauchery of overindulgence in alcohol and food. The Bible does not say as much about gluttony as about alcohol consumption, but the fact is that we can dig our graves with our teeth by overeating as well as by the abuse of alcohol or other narcotics. **Be not among** is a reminder of the influence of peer pressure. Those who hang around with people who drink will be pressured to imbibe with them.

3. The Effects of Drunkenness (Prov. 23:21,29-30)

Proverbs warns that drunkards and gluttons will experience poverty and become listless. The results of their overindulgence will be woe, sorrow, strife, complaints, bruises, and bloodshot eyes. Some fun!

Verses 21,29-30: **For the drunkard and the glutton shall come to poverty: and drowsiness shall clothe a man with rags. . . . Who hath woe? who hath sorrow? who hath contentions? who hath babbling? who hath wounds without cause? who hath redness of eyes? They that tarry long at the wine; they that go to seek mixed wine.**

Here is a graphic description of the results of drunkenness. Again **the drunkard** and **the glutton** are listed together. Those who live only for bacchanalian feasts will wind up in poverty. Not only do they waste their money, but their overindulgence also mars their capacity to earn a living—in many cases they lose their jobs because they are not dependable. Alcohol is one of the worst culprits for diminished capacity in the workplace. **Drowsiness** probably refers to the hangover following drunkenness.

The series of questions in verse 29 suggests the riddle method of teaching (Tate, "Proverbs," 75). **Woe** and **sorrow** describe the state of mind and body following a drunken bout. **Contentions** ("strife," NIV) describes one's state while drunk. **Babbling** denotes senseless talk (the NIV reads "complaints"). **Wounds** ("needless bruises," NIV) suggests hurts such as falling down because of the loss of equilibrium. **Redness of eyes** refers to one's appearance following a drunken spree. Duane A. Garrett pointed out that this expression, in addition to being translated "bloodshot eyes" (NIV), also could be rendered "blackened eyes" from beatings or "dull eyes" from blurred vision ("Proverbs," in *The New American Commentary,* vol. 14 [Nashville: Broadman Press, 1993], 197). The obvious answer to all the questions raised in verse 29 is: **They that tarry long at the wine; they that go to seek mixed wine.** In other words, "The one who consumes excessive amounts of alcohol." **Mixed wine** was wine mixed with water, honey, and spices (Tate, "Proverbs," 75). We would refer to it as "mixed drinks."

Oh, how different the sentiment of Lady Nancy Astor, who said, "When I have a good time, I want to know about it" (Ely, *I Quote,* 331).

4. The Dangerous Deception of Alcohol (Prov. 23:31-32)

One of the fascinations about alcoholic beverages and mixed drinks is that they look so pretty. They have an appealing, seductive appearance. But looks are deceiving!

Verses 31-32: **Look not thou upon the wine when it is red, when it giveth his color in the cup, when it moveth itself aright. At the last it biteth like a serpent, and stingeth like an adder.**

Verse 31 focuses on both the pleasures of the eye and the pleasures of the taste of alcoholic beverages. The *New International Version* gives a better translation of verse 31. "Do not gaze at wine when it is red, when it sparkles in the cup, when it goes down smoothly!"

Look not thou upon the wine when it is red. There is no harm, of course, merely in *gazing* at wine–whether its color is red, blush, or white. The prohibitory reference about **red** wine refers either to wine's ability to fascinate the onlooker so that in no time one is imbibing it or to the wine's potency.

Sparkling wine and fancy mixed drinks have an enticing power. William McKane warned, "There is a fatal fascination for the eyes in red wine sparkling in the cup." Thus, you must not "allow yourself to be hypnotized by the rich color of red wine" (*Proverbs,* in The Old Testament Library [Philadelphia: The Westminster Press, 1970], 394). Television commercials and advertisements for sparkling wine, mixed drinks, and beer make this fact abundantly clear. Deceptively attractive and misleading advertising by the makers of beverage alcohol presents a great challenge believers need to address in educating people to the dangers of consuming alcohol.

On the other hand, **red** wine may refer to undiluted or unmixed wine that had a greater alcohol content. In Jesus' time the rabbis had formulas for diluting wine, so much water for a given wine. Wine from Lebanon was noted for its potency and required more water to dilute than some other wines. The resultant product had a stimulus about like coffee or tea. This was the wine used at meals, the wine that Jesus drank. Thus, in drinking red wine one received the full alcoholic content.

People falsely may think alcohol is harmless, but they need to recognize its deadly potential. Such beverages go down the throat smoothly, but once in the bloodstream they are most vicious. They bite like a **serpent** with its poisonous fangs. They sting like an **adder**–the adder's sting being poisonous. The adder probably should be identified with the *Daboia Xanthina.* This particular snake is "a highly venomous viper and the largest snake of Palestine. It has been described as the most dreaded serpent mentioned in the Old Testament" (Tate, "Proverbs," 75).

One of the greatest dangers of alcohol and other drugs is that they create an increased appetite for themselves. Drinks with a low alcohol content and other similar narcotics soon fail to satisfy. Then the body calls for such with increased strength. Before one knows it, he or she has gone from wine coolers and lite beer to the hardest of liquors or stronger drugs. And before one realizes it, he or she is enslaved by it. Alcohol and narcotics have a vicious nature. A child, youth, or older person may take a light dose as a lark; but before one knows it, he or she is on the hard stuff, for the weaker soon does not satisfy. The only safe thing is to say *NO!* at the outset—and stick with it.

5. The Results of Addiction to Alcohol (Prov. 23:33-35)

Verses 33-35: **Thine eyes shall behold strange women, and thine heart shall utter perverse things. Yea, thou shalt be as he that lieth down in the midst of the sea, or as he that lieth upon the top of a mast. They have stricken me, shalt thou say, and I was not sick; they have beaten me; and I felt it not: when shall I awake? I will seek it yet again.**

These verses picture graphically the effects of drunkenness. A better reading for **thine eyes shall behold strange women** is "your eyes will see strange sights" (NIV). This speaks of hallucinations. **Thine heart shall utter perverse things** may better read "and your mind imagine confusing things" (NIV). Literally, the Hebrew reads, "your mind will speak things which are upside down" (Tate, "Proverbs," 75).

Verses 34-35 are picturesque. They offer a comic but sad picture of the alcoholic's condition. Everything around a drunkard seems to be moving and tossing. His equilibrium is almost nil. So the wise man likens him to someone who **lieth down in the midst of the sea,** that is, who makes his bed in the sea. The sea is never still. Continuing with the nautical image, the drunkard also is likened to one who lies down **upon the top of a mast**—the roughest place of all on a ship. The ship's least movement causes the mast to swing back and forth in an exaggerated way. But there is more involved in this figure than just the rocking and swaying motion. The drunkard's situation is precarious and critical. Only one small slip and he's a goner. "The drunkard is, indeed, thus often exposed to the peril of his life;

for an accident of itself not great, or a stroke, may suddenly put an end to his life" (Franz Delitzsch, "The Book of Proverbs," *Biblical Commentary on the Old Testament* [Grand Rapids: William B. Eerdmans Publishing Co., 1970 reprint], 124).

The drunkard's mind is so benumbed by alcohol that if someone strikes him he feels no pain. **They have stricken me . . . they have beaten me,** he reported, **and I felt it not.** The delicate brain is the communication center for the entire body. What utter folly that anyone would abuse it thus!

In the midst of his agonizing and fitful tossing, a fleeting second of awareness leads him to question—**When shall I awake** from this nightmare of torture? Eventually, he does awaken. And what is the first thing he does? He reaches for his bottle, determined **I will seek it yet again.** The very thing that got him in that fix he clutches to his bosom as if it were his dearest friend. The cycle goes on and on. Indeed, "before one hangover is finished, the alcoholic is anticipating drinking again" (Tate, "Proverbs," 75). If another person did to him what the bottle did, he would regard that person as a mortal enemy. He would avoid him or her as he would a plague—yet he reaches out for the bottle again!

Alcohol has powerful effects on the lives of people. It can make them scoffers, involve them in physical violence, and rob them of mental and physical coordination. People who indulge in the consumption of alcoholic beverages and illegal drugs experience a variety of physical and emotional difficulties. Too often these people falsely think that alcohol is harmless. They need to recognize its deadly potential. Addiction to alcohol and drugs distorts their view of reality. As a matter of fact, many people who are addicted are unaware of their true condition. Thus, instead of seeking help, they foolishly seek more alcohol or stronger drugs. The biblically wise person does not do this. The wise person demonstrates his or her wisdom by abstaining from the consumption of alcohol and illegal drugs, and thus avoids the dangers of alcohol and illegal drugs.